MISTRESS OF THE MOON I

A TRIBUTE TO THE MOON COLORING BOOK

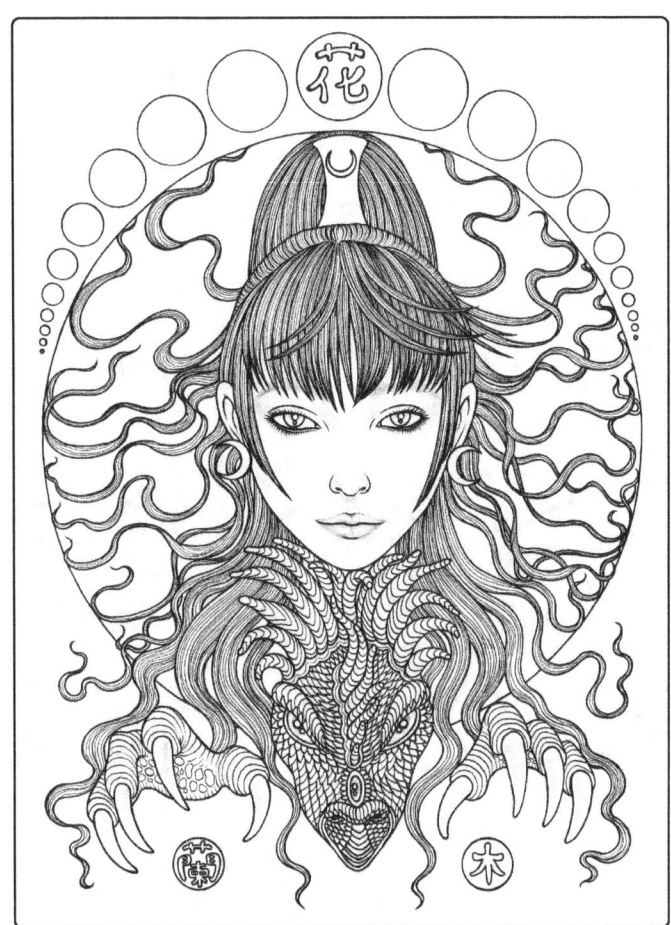

2 x 20 Hand Drawn Illustrations by Wheeshan Ong

Includes 2 each of 20 Images (One Black & White, One Light Gray)

First Published November 2019
ISBN: 9781705859612

www.wheeshanong.com

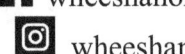

wheeshanong

wheeshan

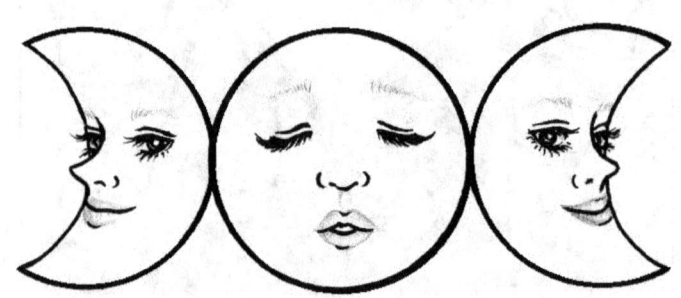

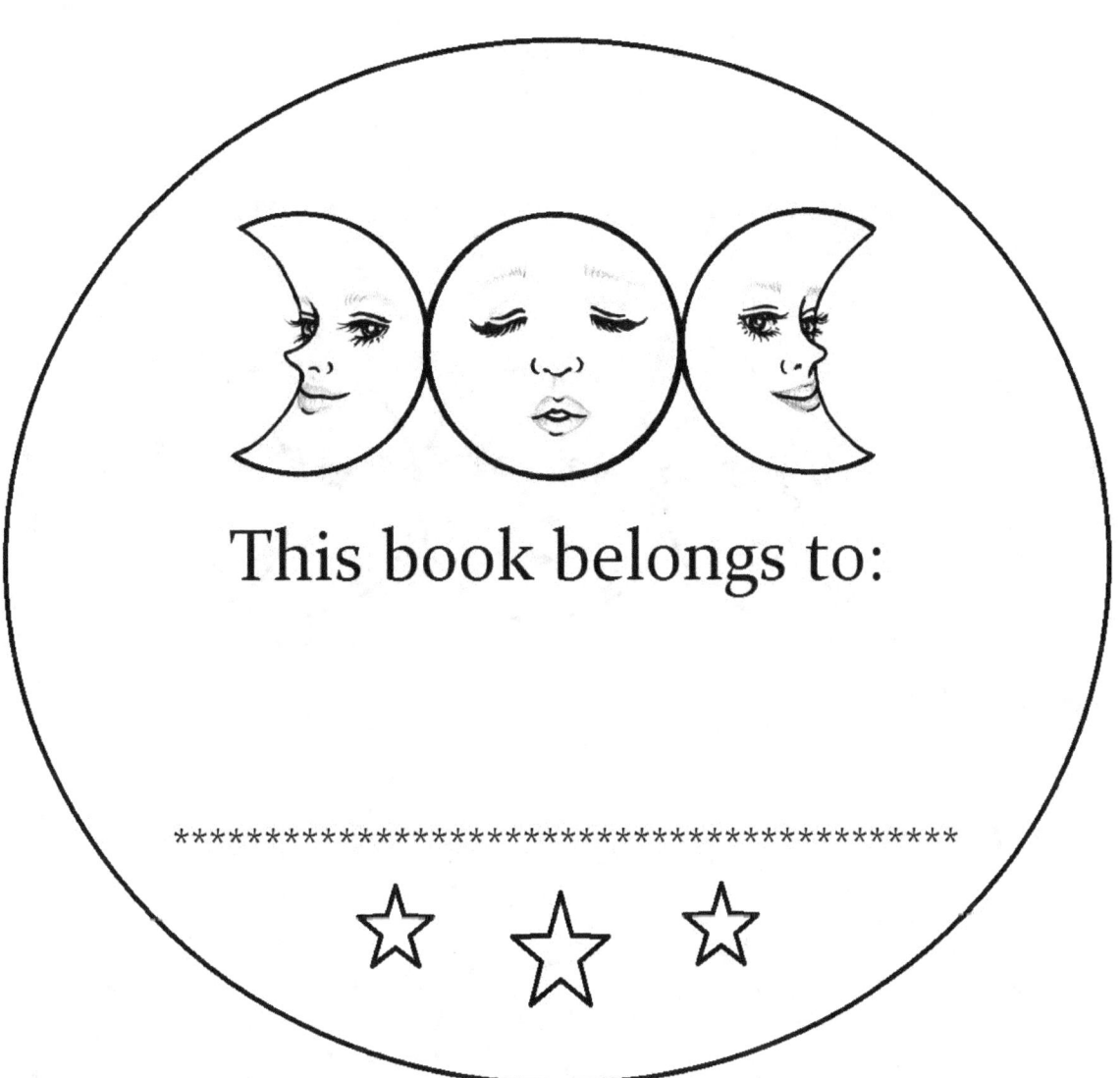

This book belongs to:

****

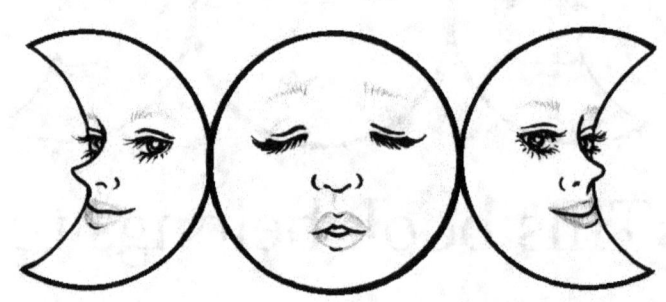

Note from the Author:

"The Moon is a reminder that no matter what phase I am in, I am still whole."

— Unknown.

I love everything about the Moon - her light, her ever changing phases, and her magic. I am enchanted by this mysterious object in the night sky. Whenever I do Moon gazing, I feel as if I am looking at a mirror, and it reflects back to me, my own essence.

One can learn a lot by observing the Moon and its cycle. Every moon phase emits a particular vibration – for e.g. new moon is good for planting seeds and starting new project; full moon is great for spiritual completion and harvest, it is also a good time for letting go of the old.

The Moon is a powerful symbol of the Divine Feminine. In different mythologies and folktales, many goddesses are often associated with the Moon.

As an artist, I find a lot of comfort and healing in drawing this archetypal symbol.

I hope that by coloring the images in this book, it will help deepen your connection with the Moon, and therefore draw you closer to the Divine Feminine within your heart.

I am dedicating this book to Grandmother Moon – the most beautiful object in the night sky. May her magic bring us hope, love, and the courage to connect with our soul.

If you like to see more of my art, please check my website - www.wheeshanong.com. You may also find me at www.instagram.com/wheeshan and www.facebook.com/wheeshanong. Do follow me to see my future creation.

You may share your colored pages in social media. Please be sure to credit me as the artist. Thank you!

Let your imaginations guide you and enjoy coloring!

"Moon Images"

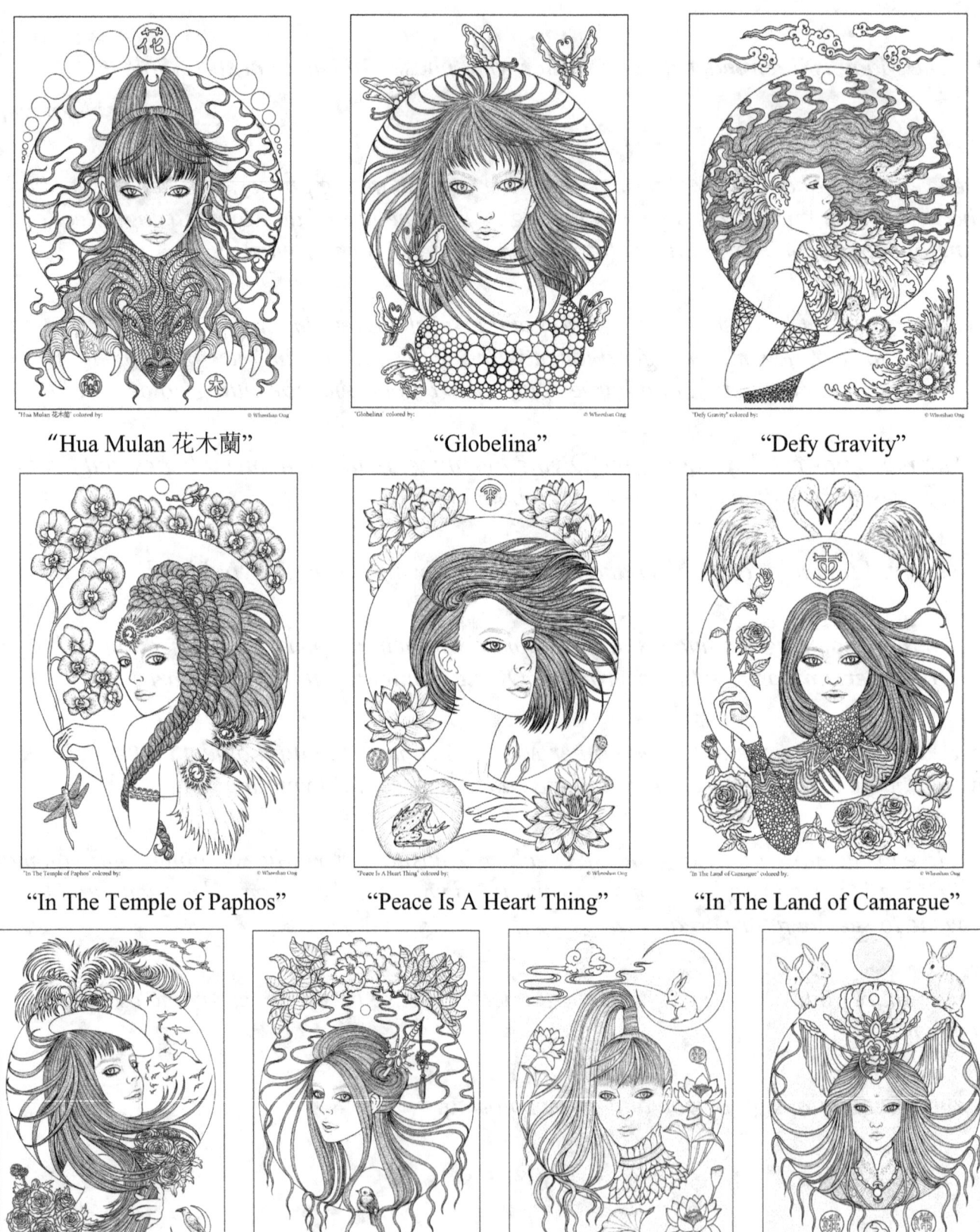

"Hua Mulan 花木蘭"

"Globelina"

"Defy Gravity"

"In The Temple of Paphos"

"Peace Is A Heart Thing"

"In The Land of Camargue"

"I Am Magic"

"Moon Is A Charmer"

"Bunny On The Moon"

"Chang'e 嫦娥"

In order of appearance - Images 1 to 10

"Moon Images"

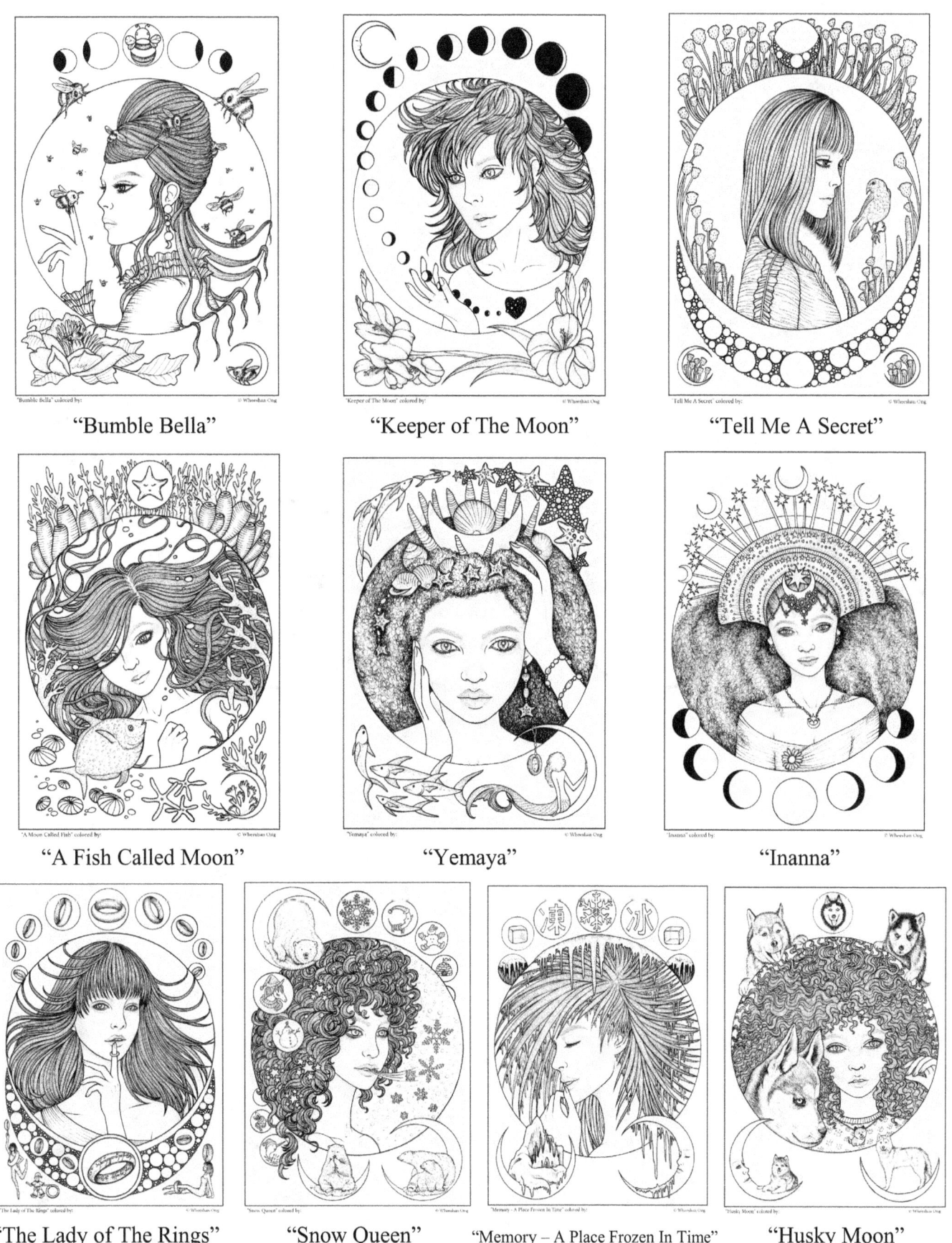

"Bumble Bella"

"Keeper of The Moon"

"Tell Me A Secret"

"A Fish Called Moon"

"Yemaya"

"Inanna"

"The Lady of The Rings"

"Snow Queen"

"Memory – A Place Frozen In Time"

"Husky Moon"

In order of appearance - Images 11 to 20

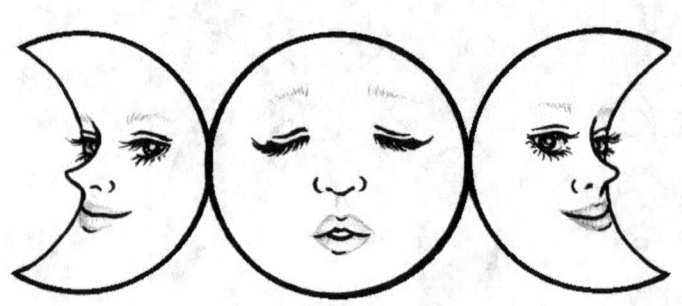

Moon Is The Magic

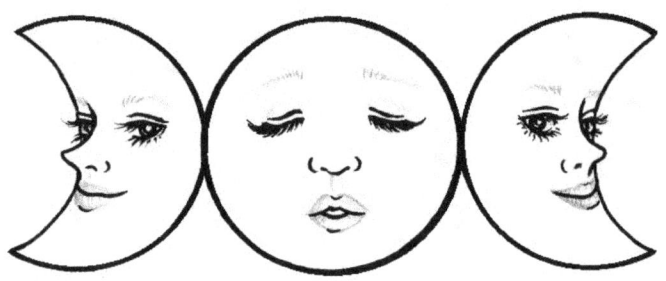

Love Is The Key

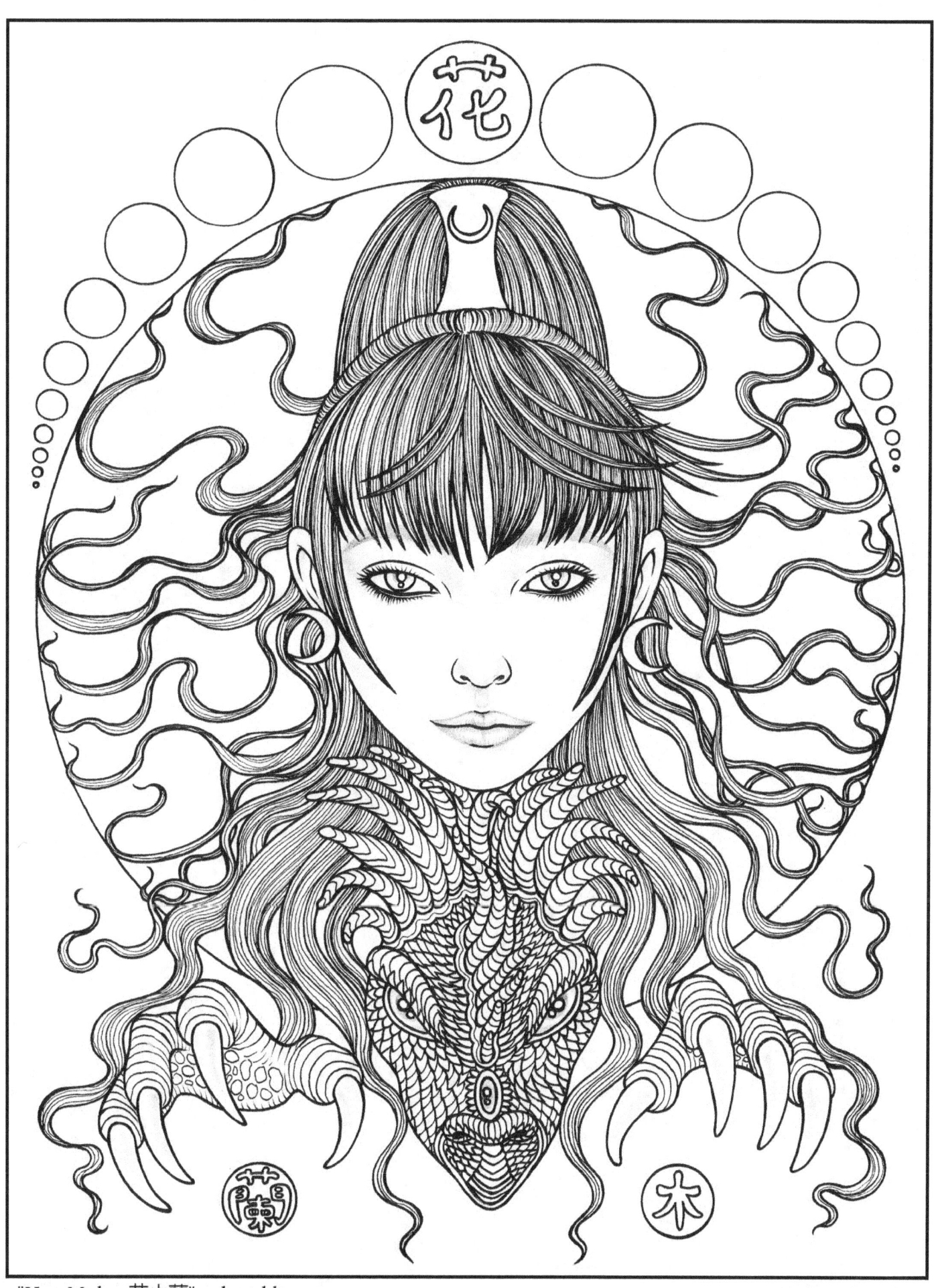

"Hua Mulan 花木蘭" colored by:

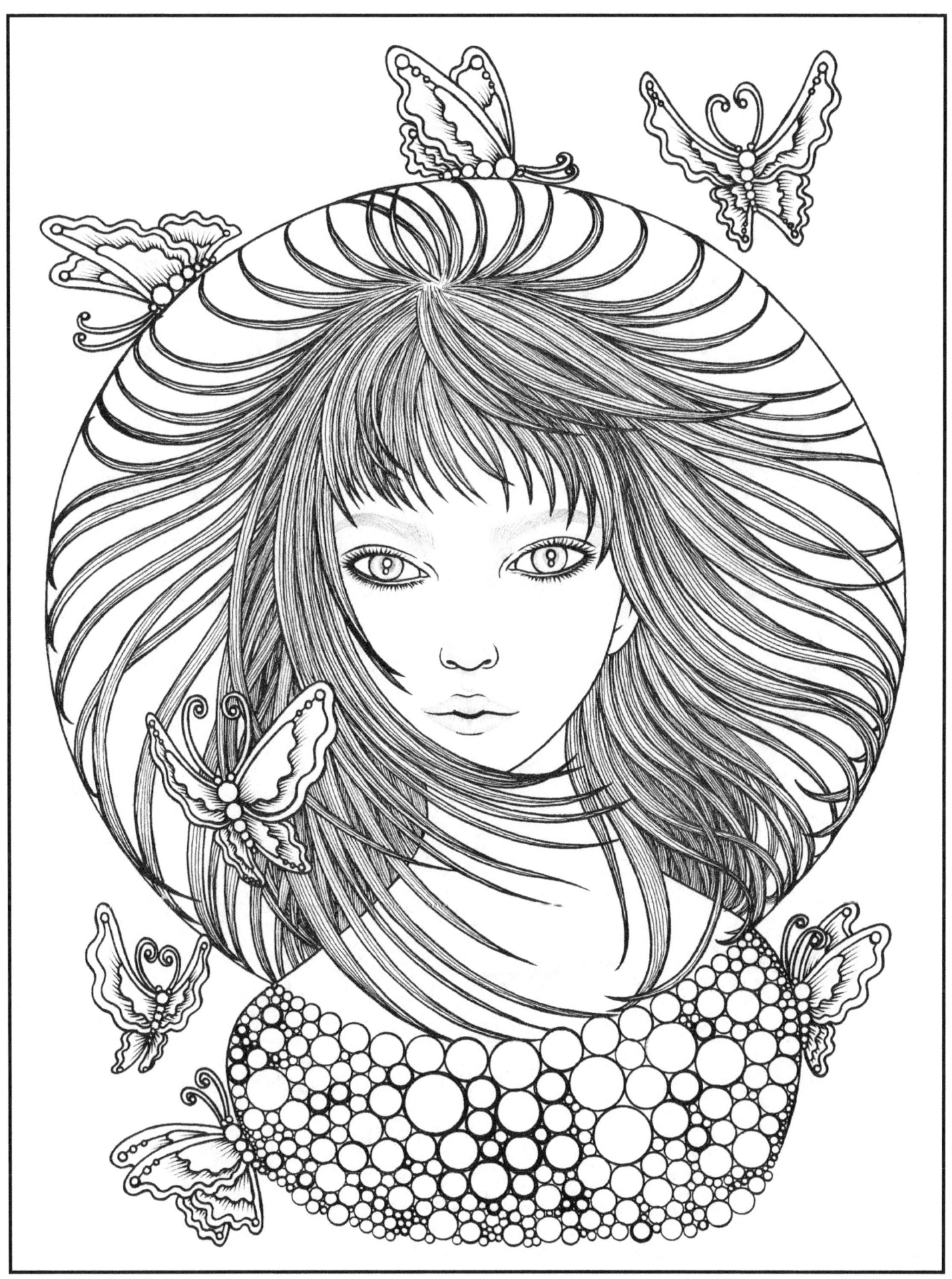

"Globelina" colored by:

© Wheeshan Ong

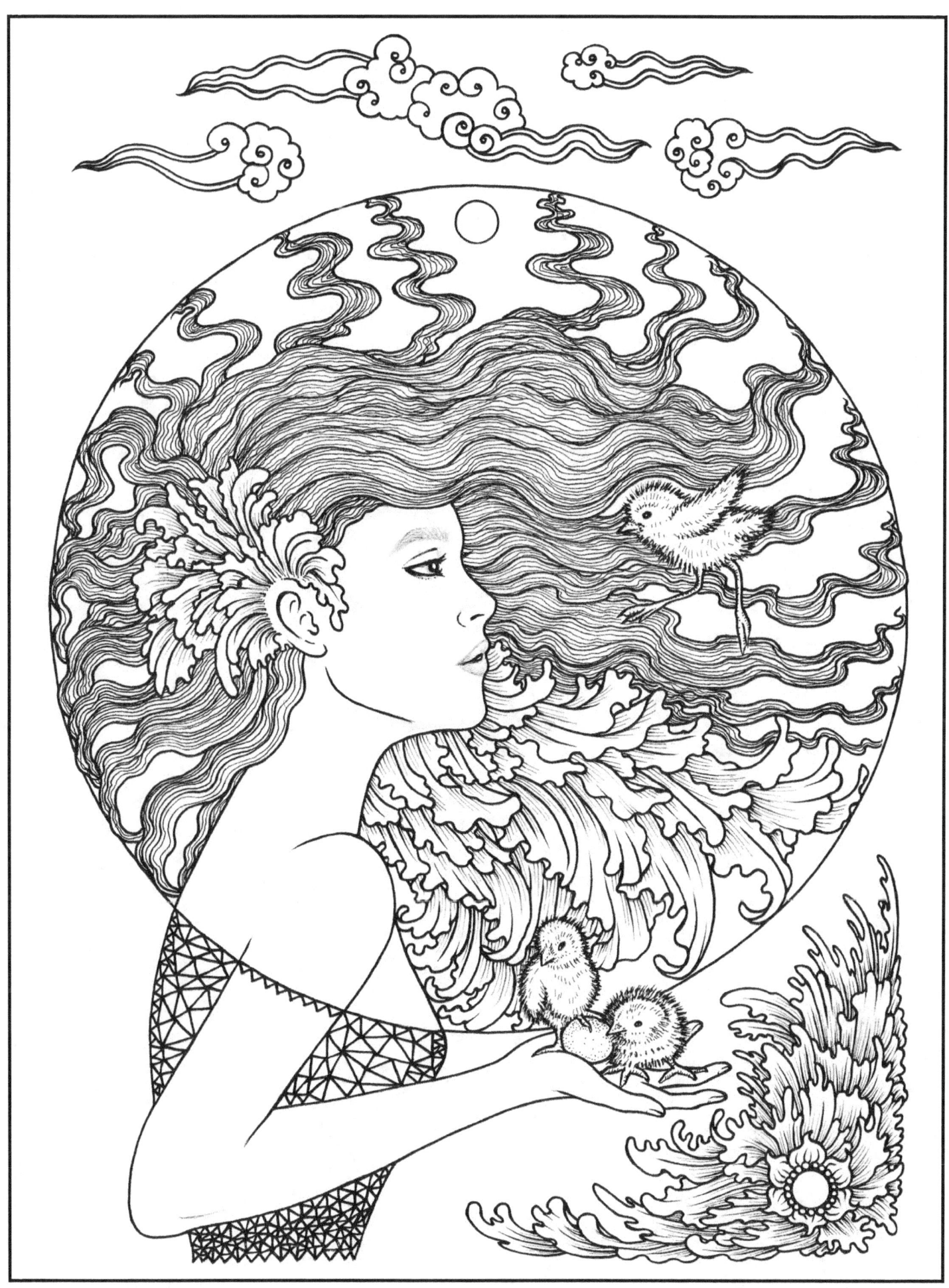

"Defy Gravity" colored by:

© Wheeshan Ong

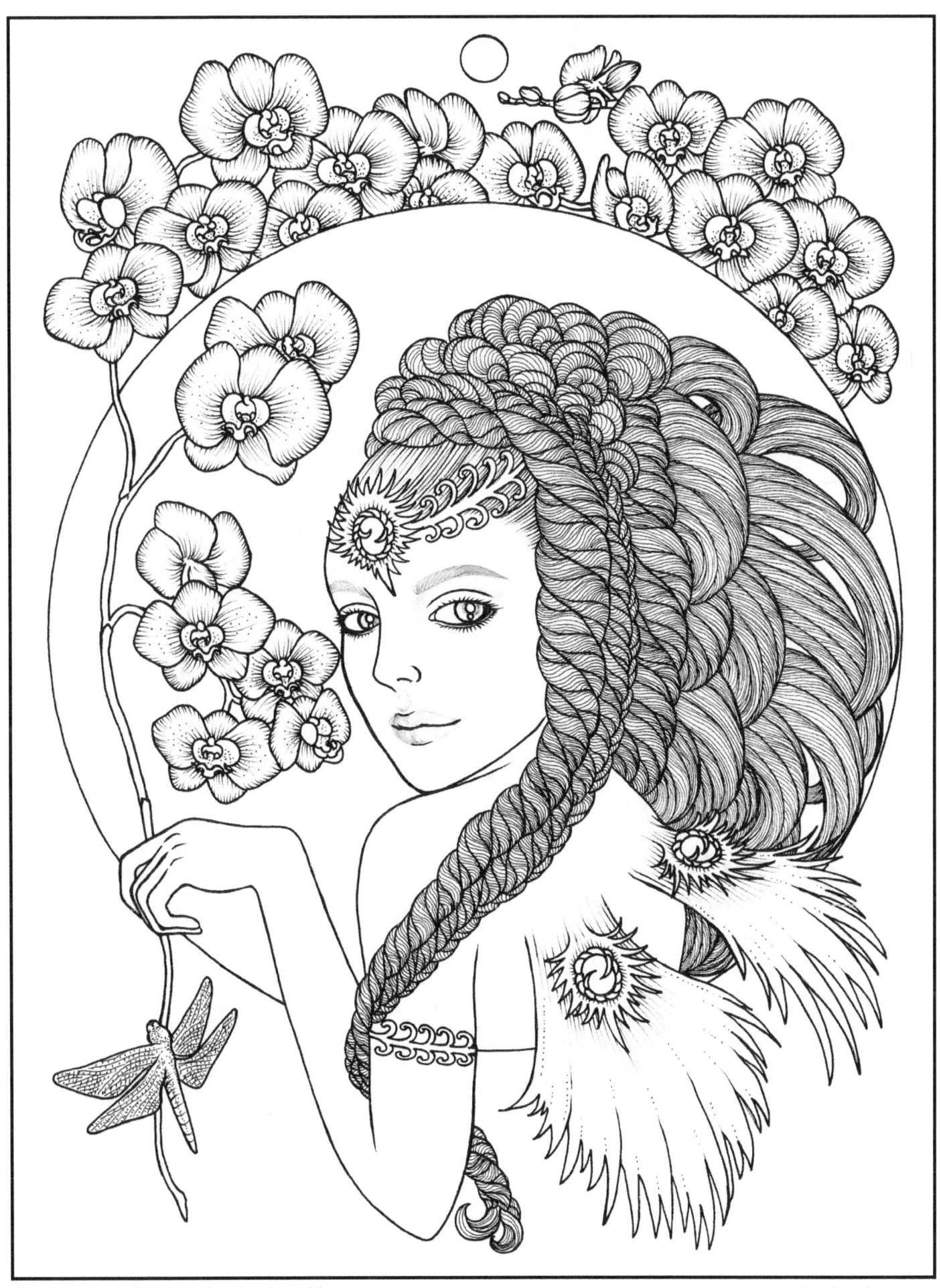

"In The Temple of Paphos" colored by:

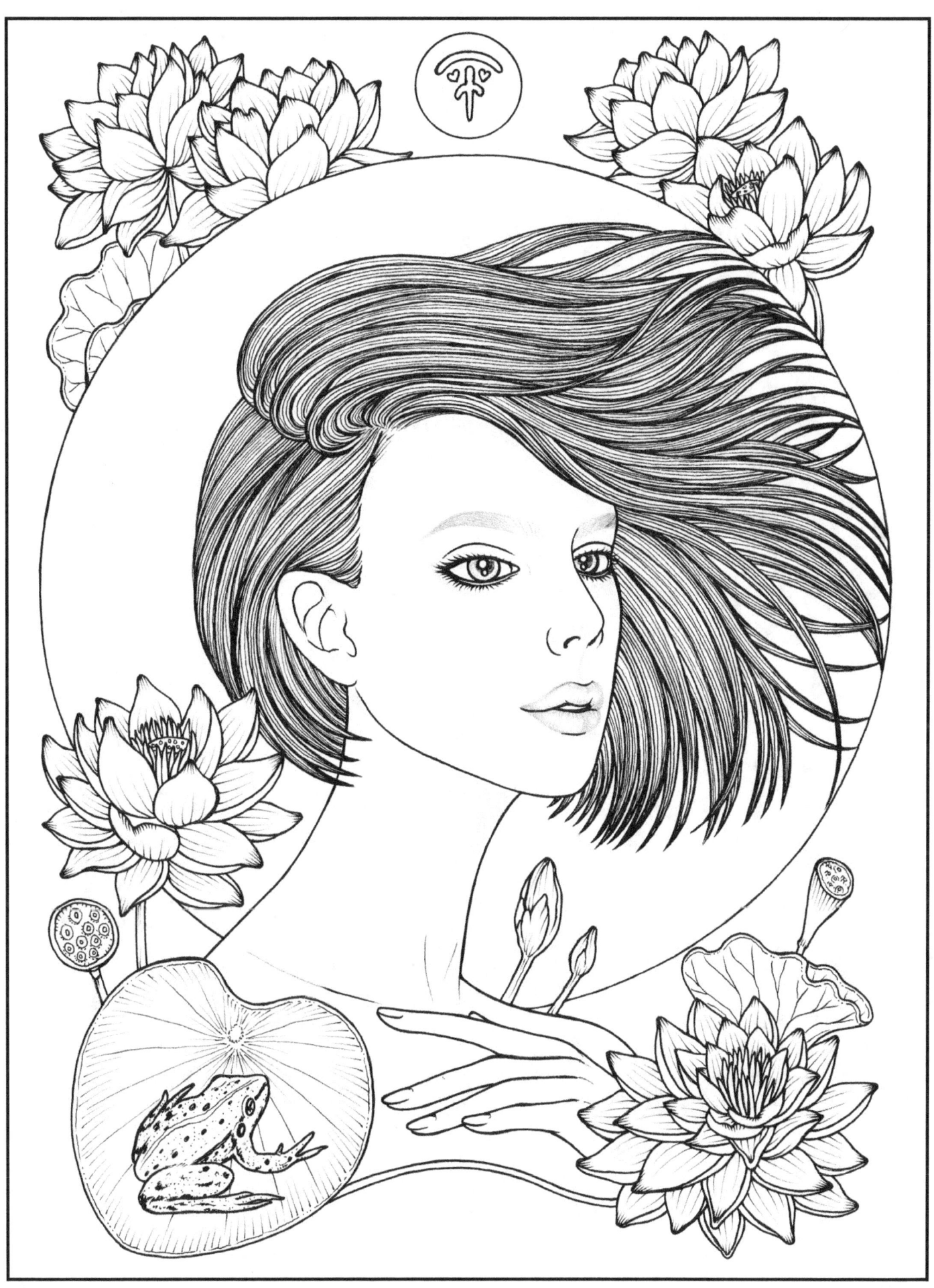

"Peace Is A Heart Thing" colored by:

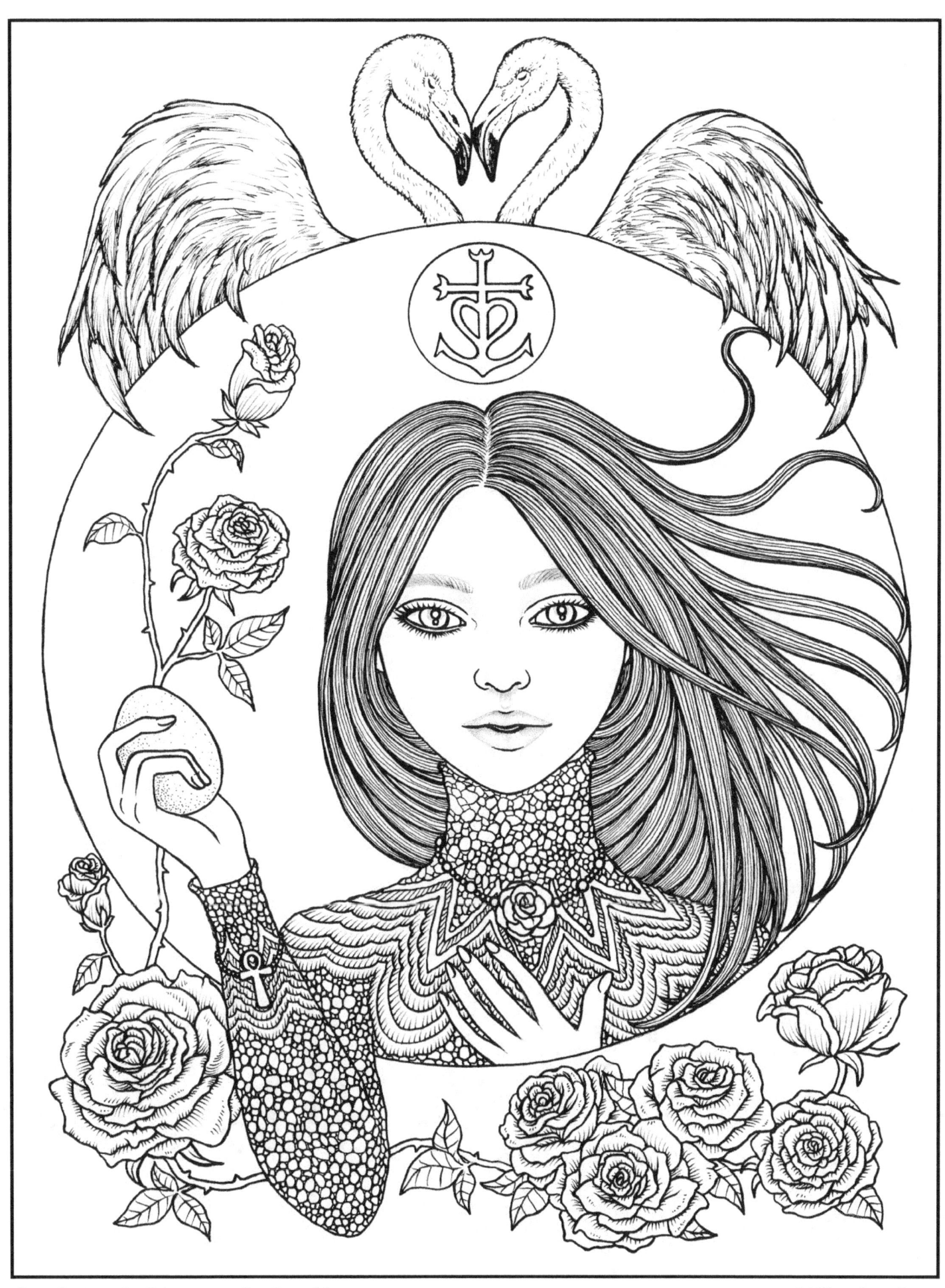

"In The Land of Camargue" colored by:

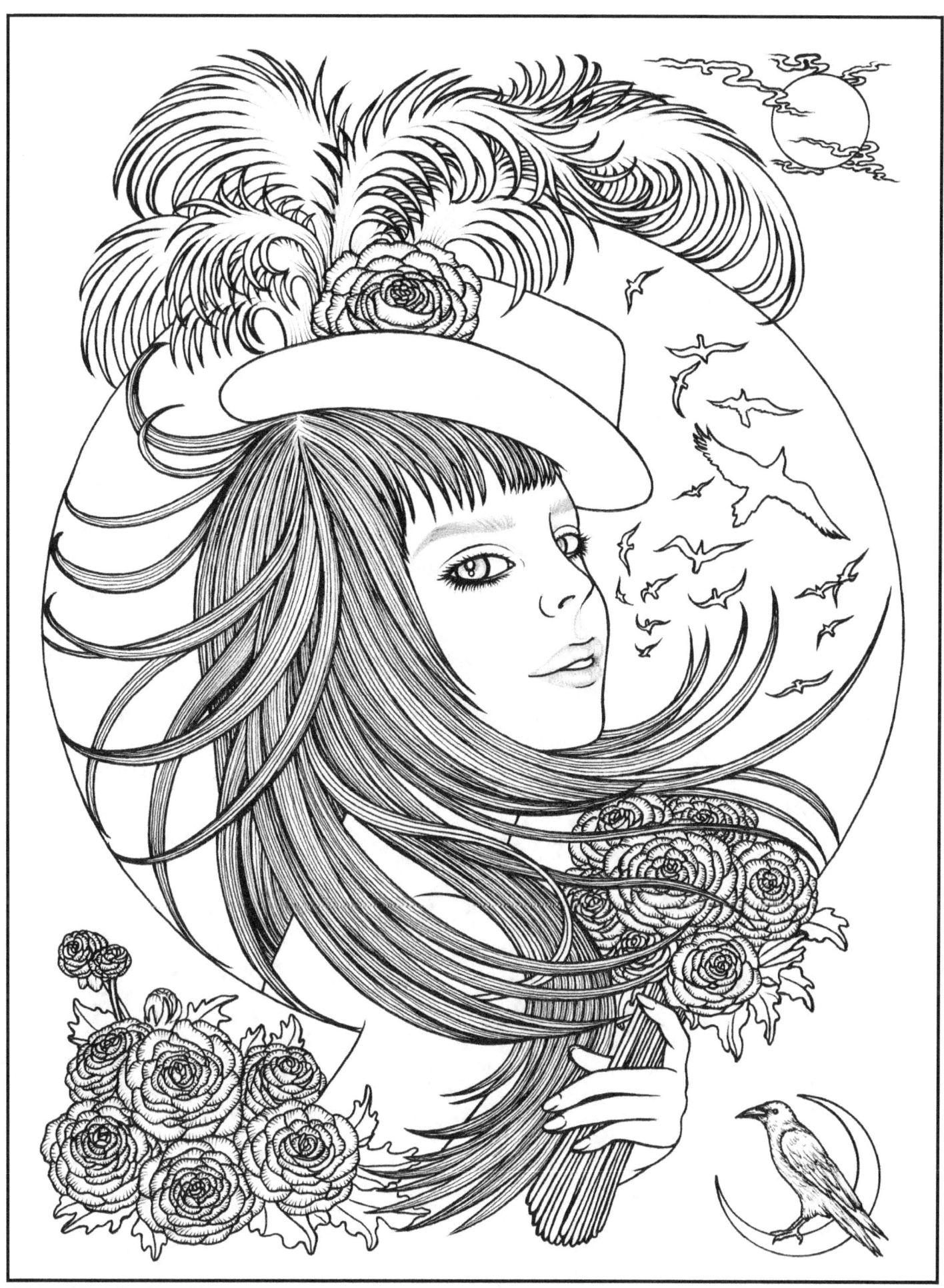

"I Am Magic" colored by:

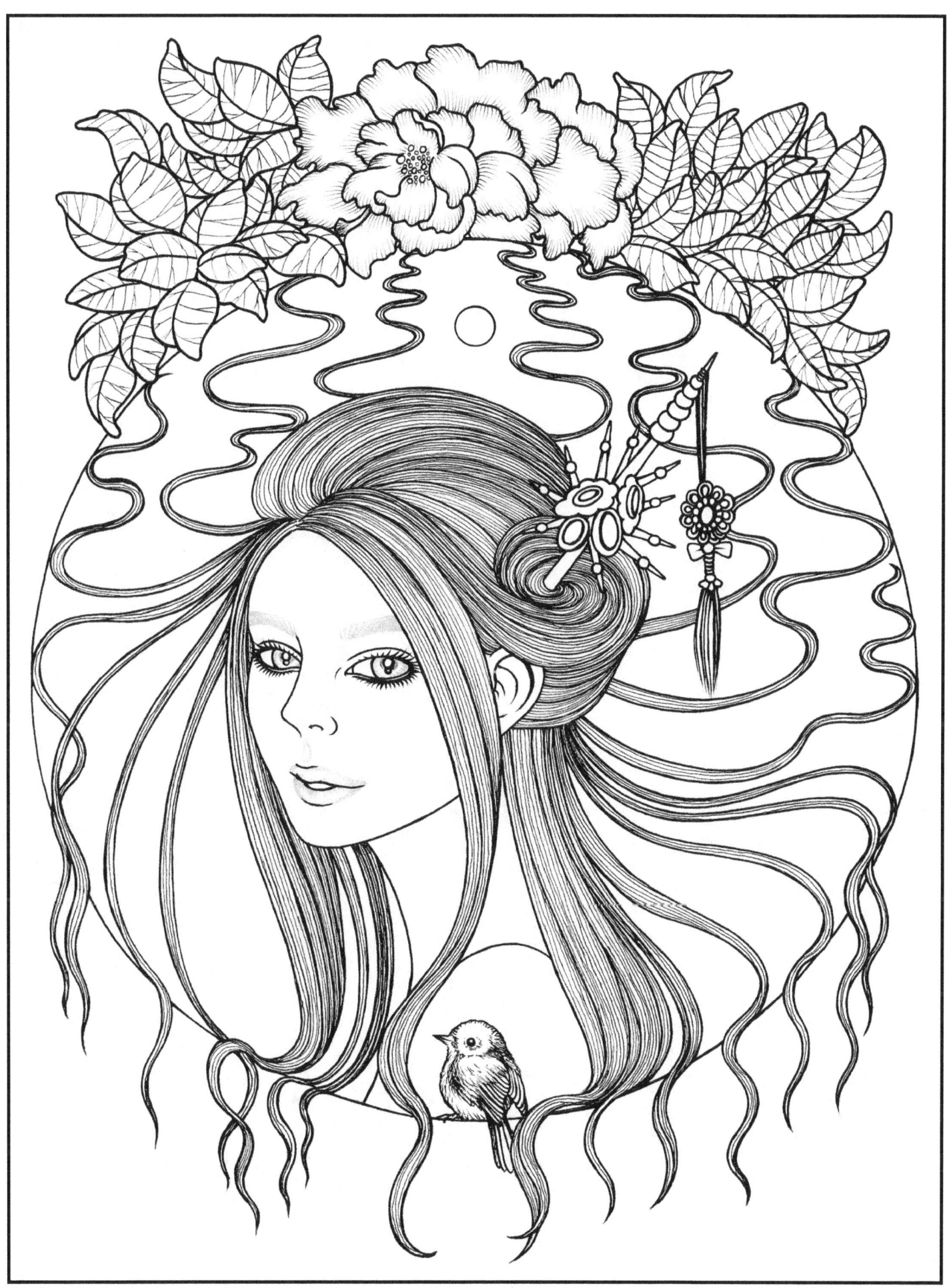

"Moon Is A Charmer" colored by:

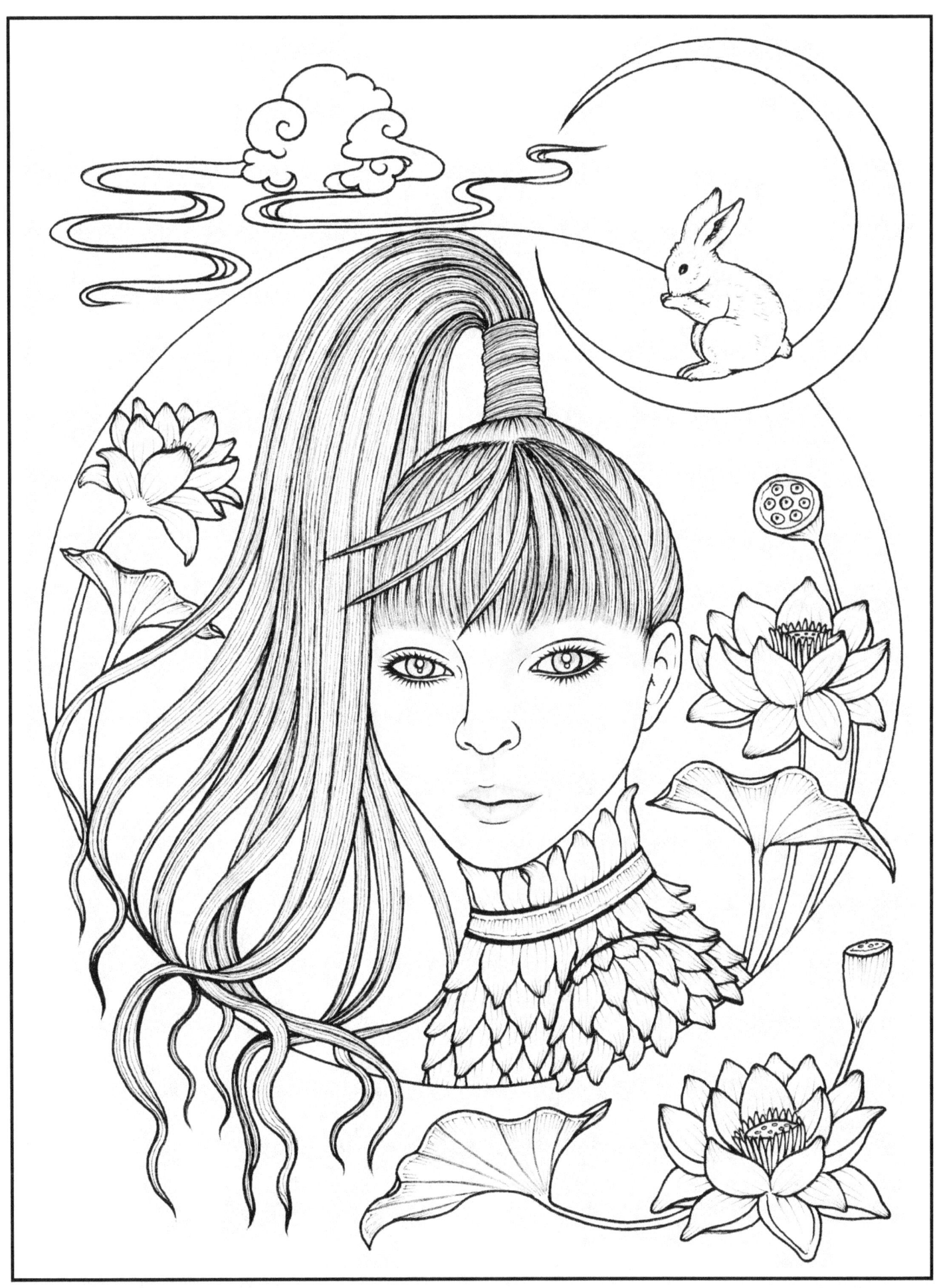

"Bunny On The Moon" colored by:

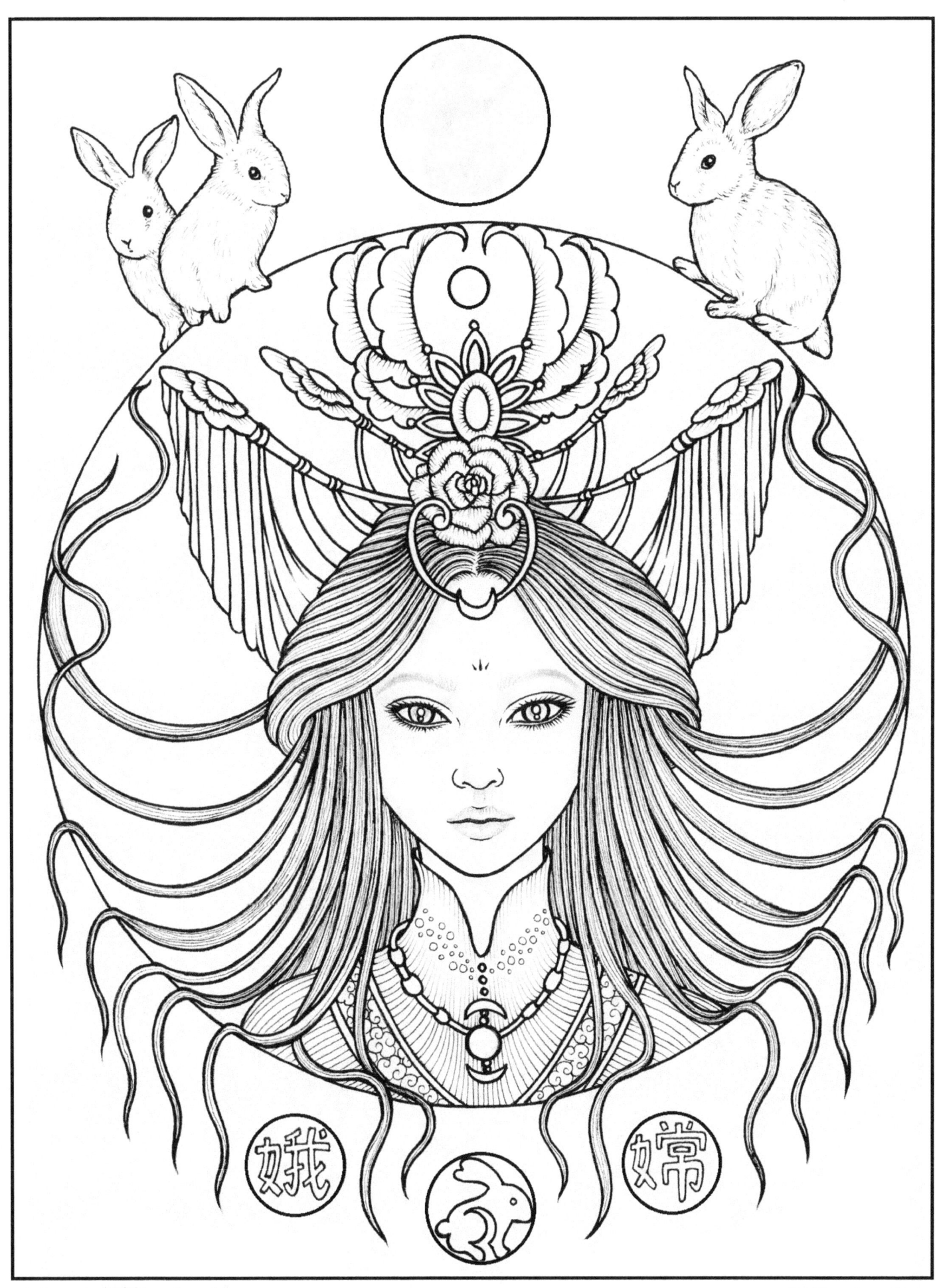

"Chang'e 嫦娥" colored by:

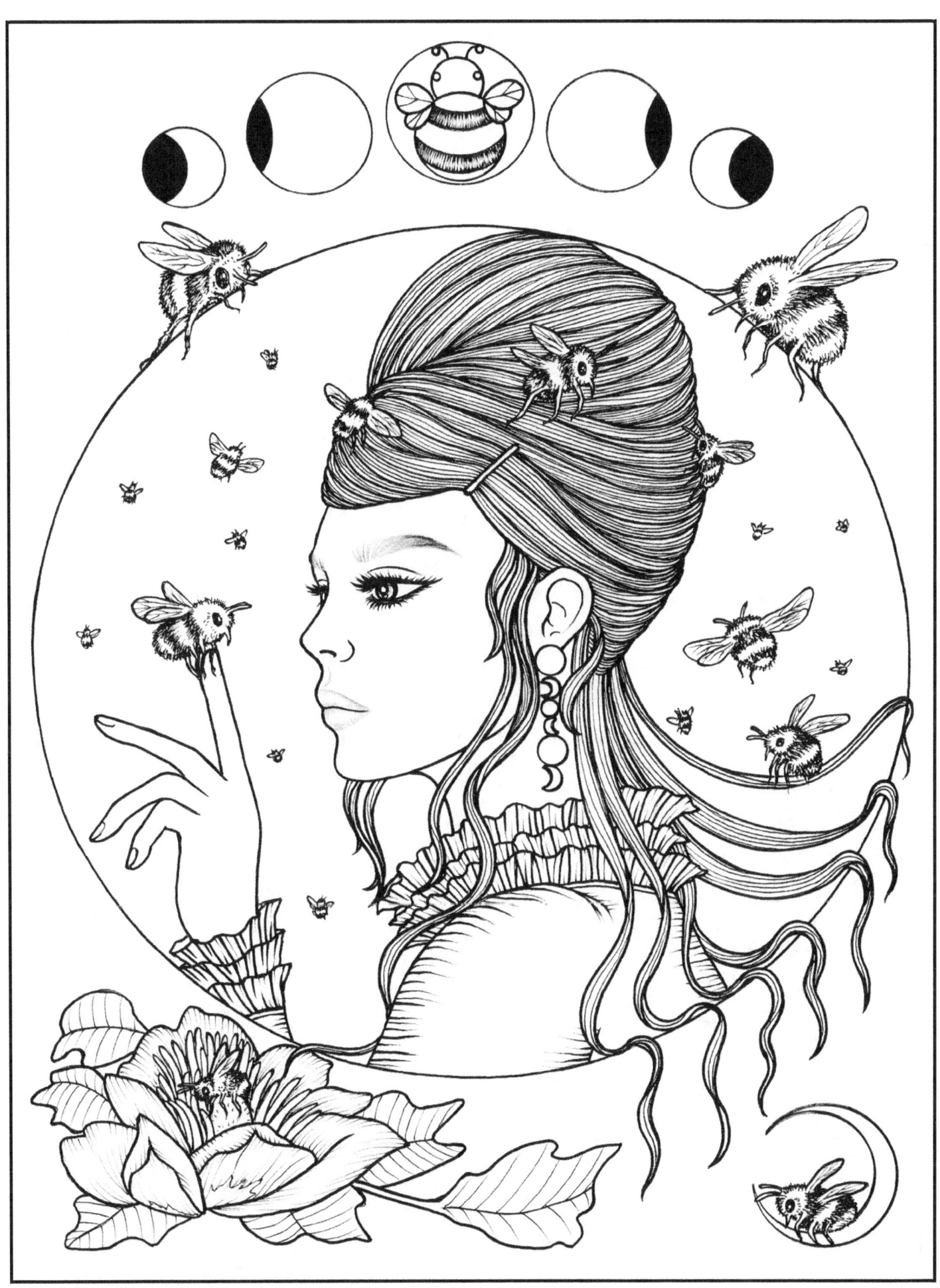

"Bumble Bella" colored by:

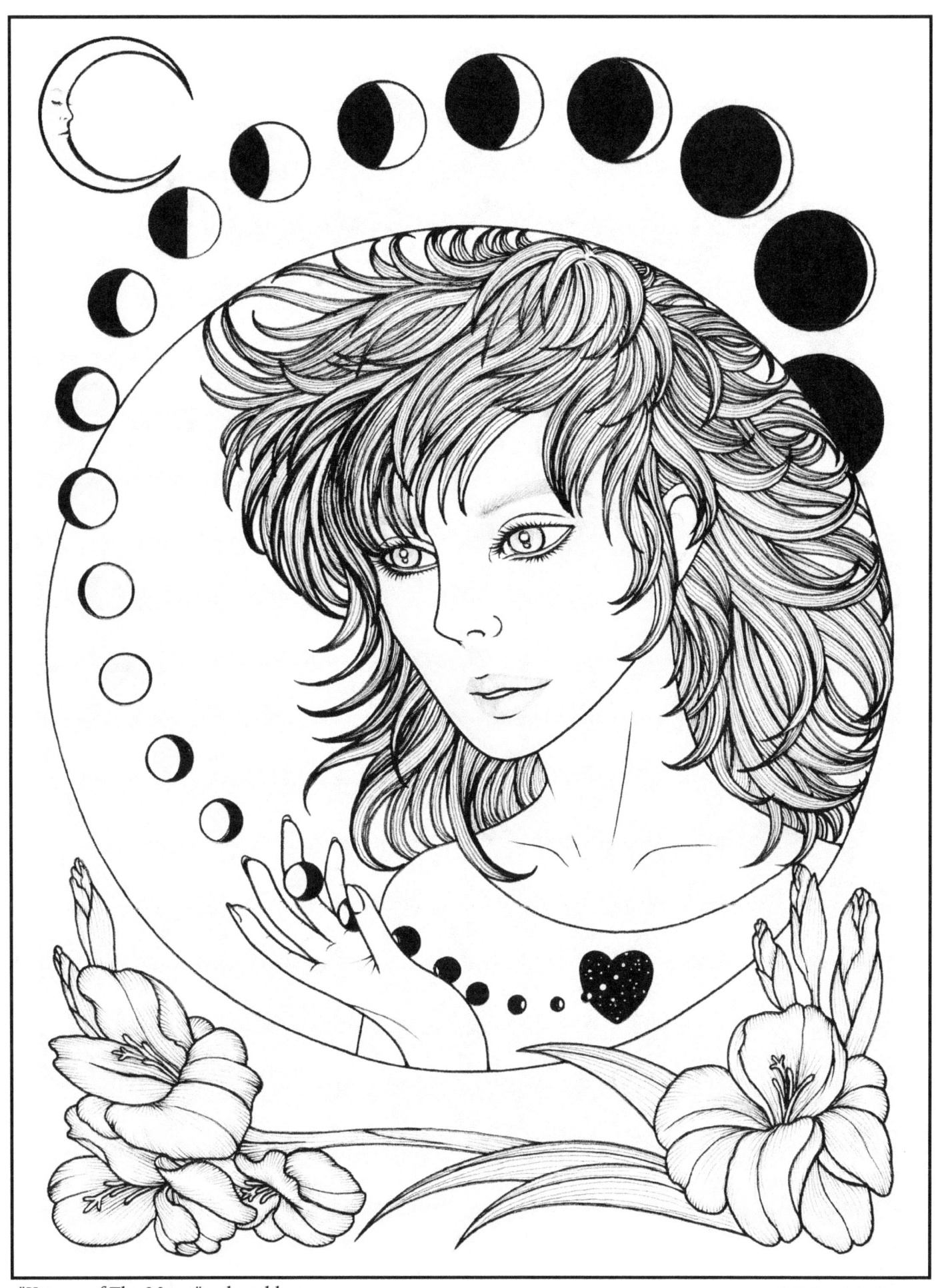

"Keeper of The Moon" colored by:

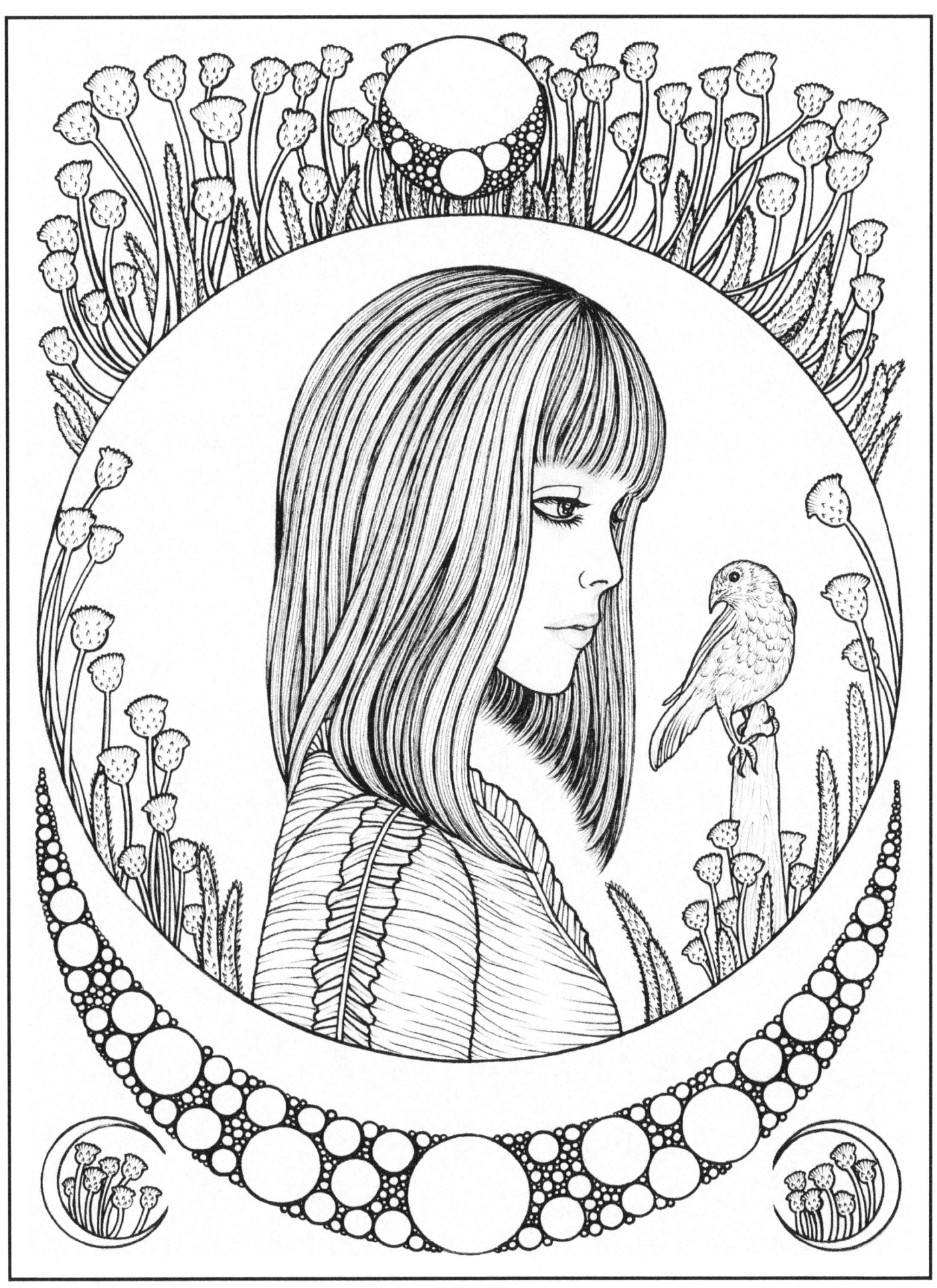

"Tell Me A Secret" colored by: © Wheeshan Ong

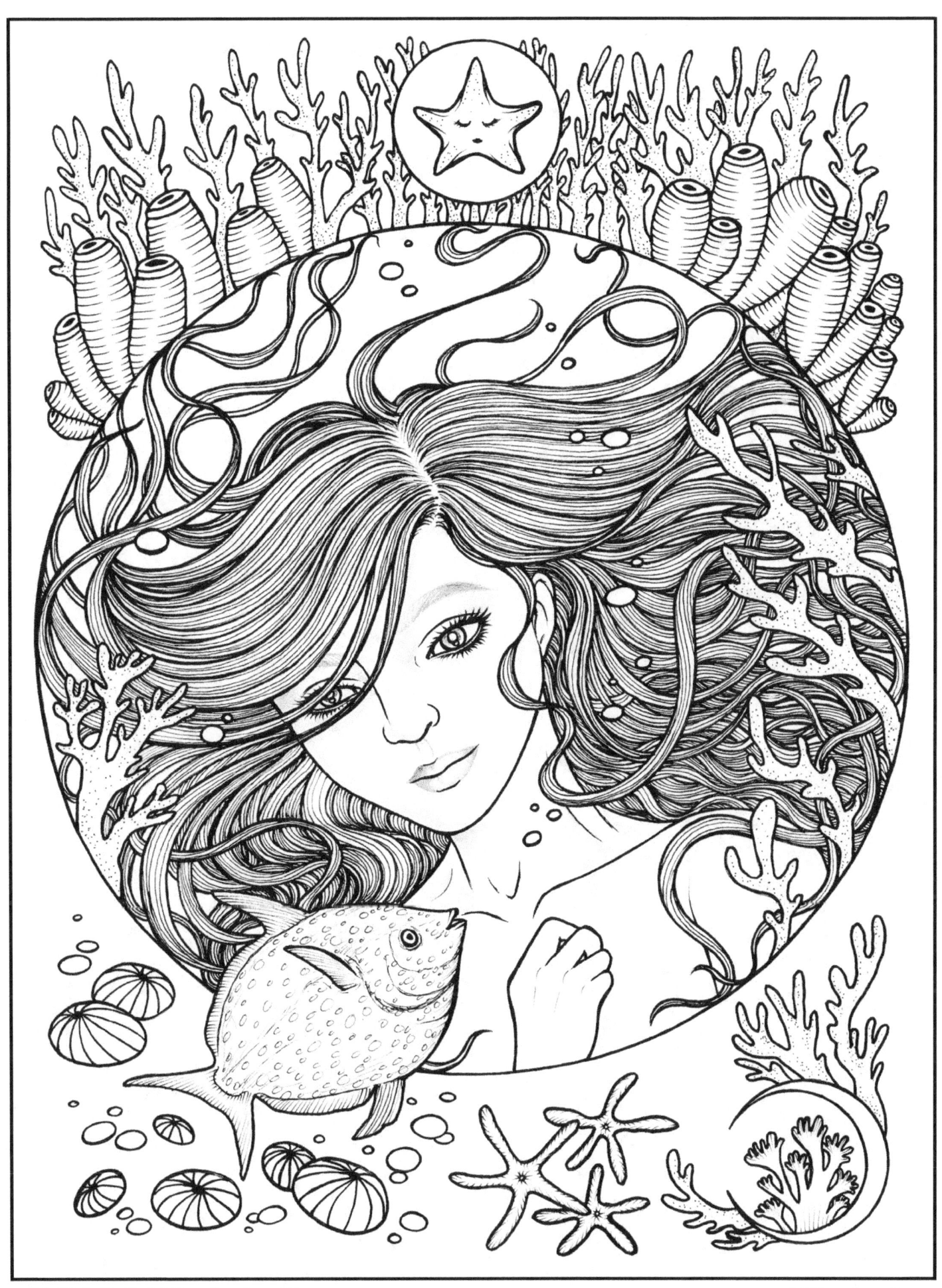

"A Fish Called Moon" colored by:

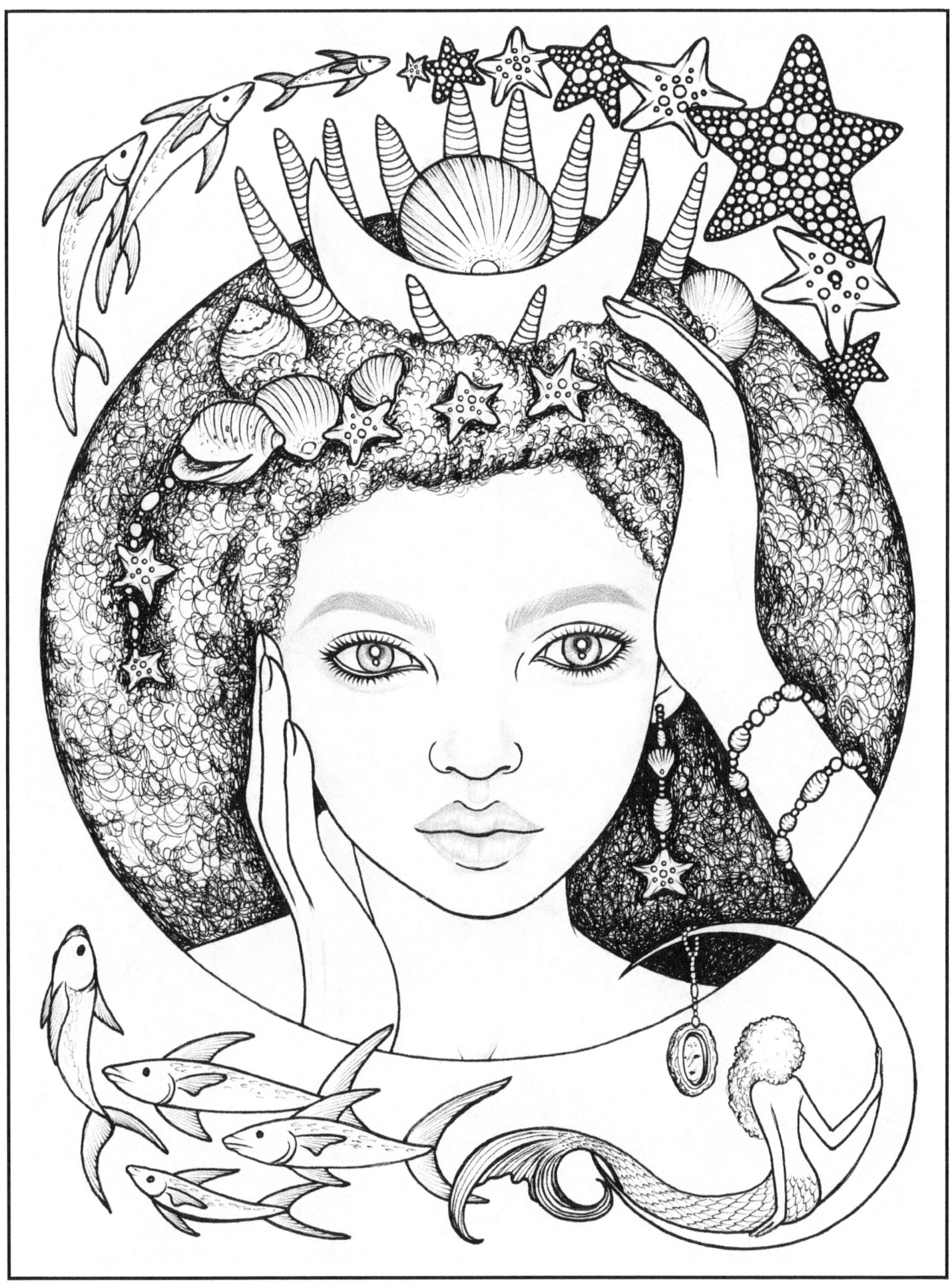

"Yemaya" colored by:

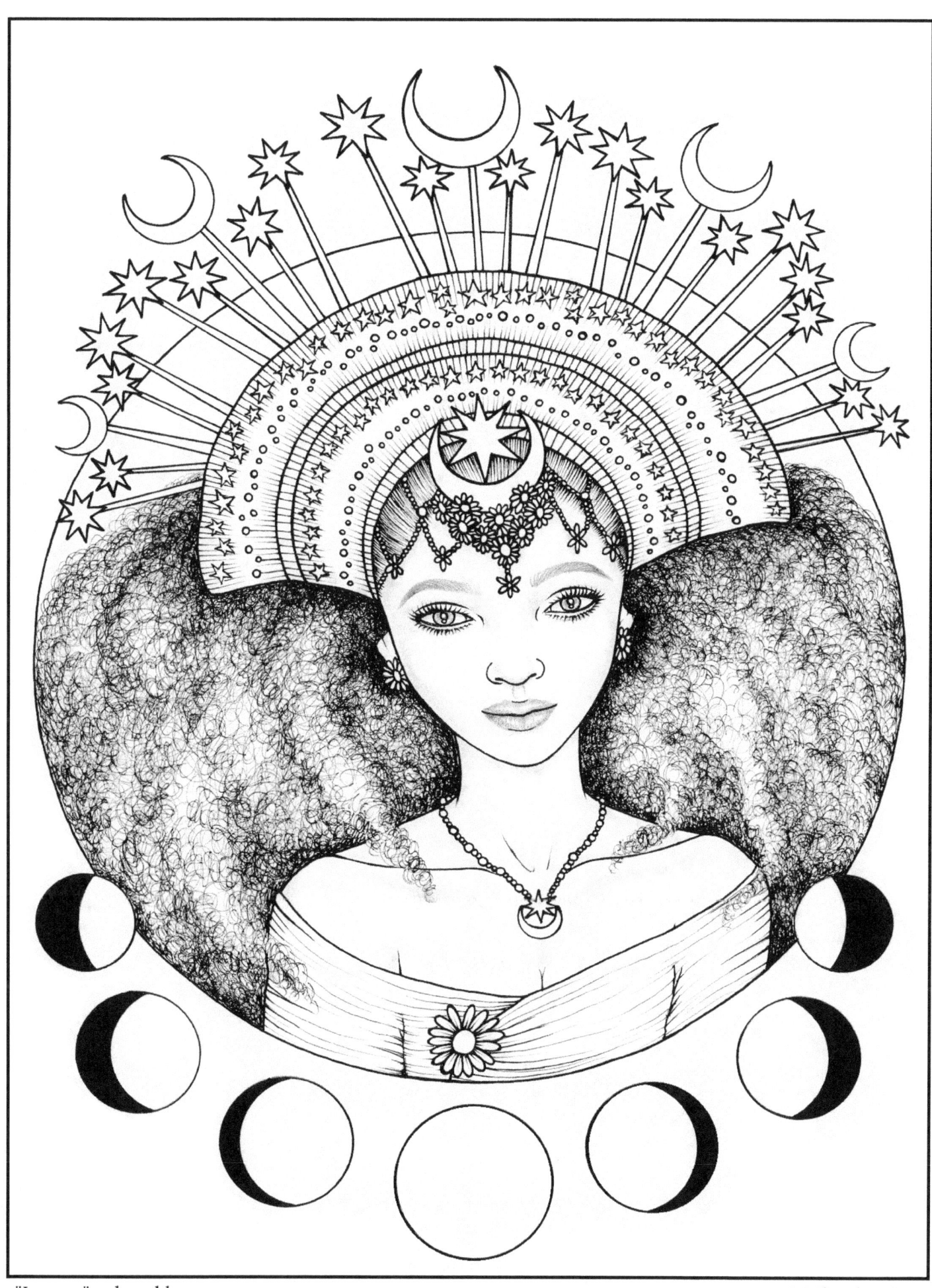

"Inanna" colored by:

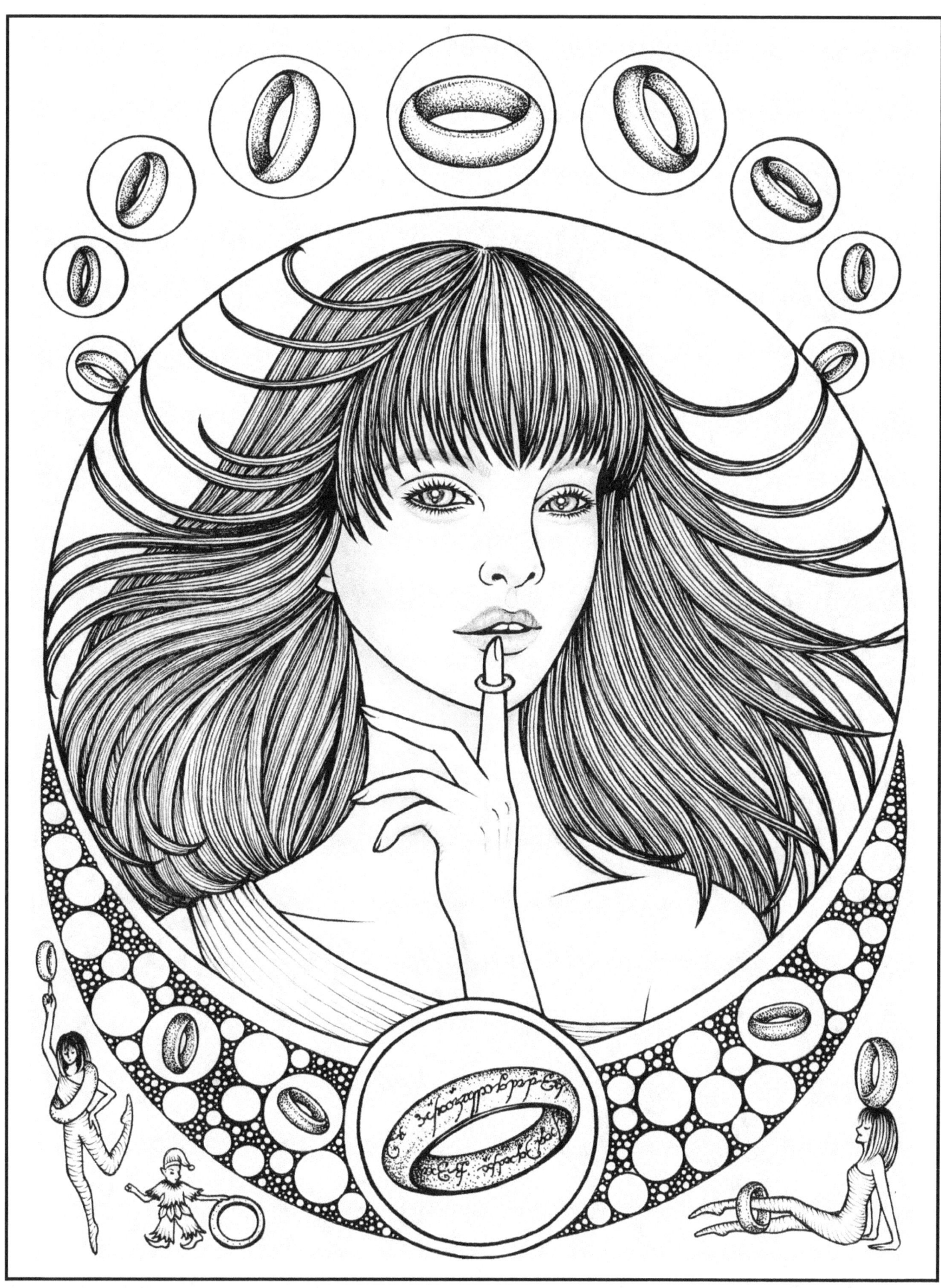

"The Lady of The Rings" colored by: © Wheeshan Ong

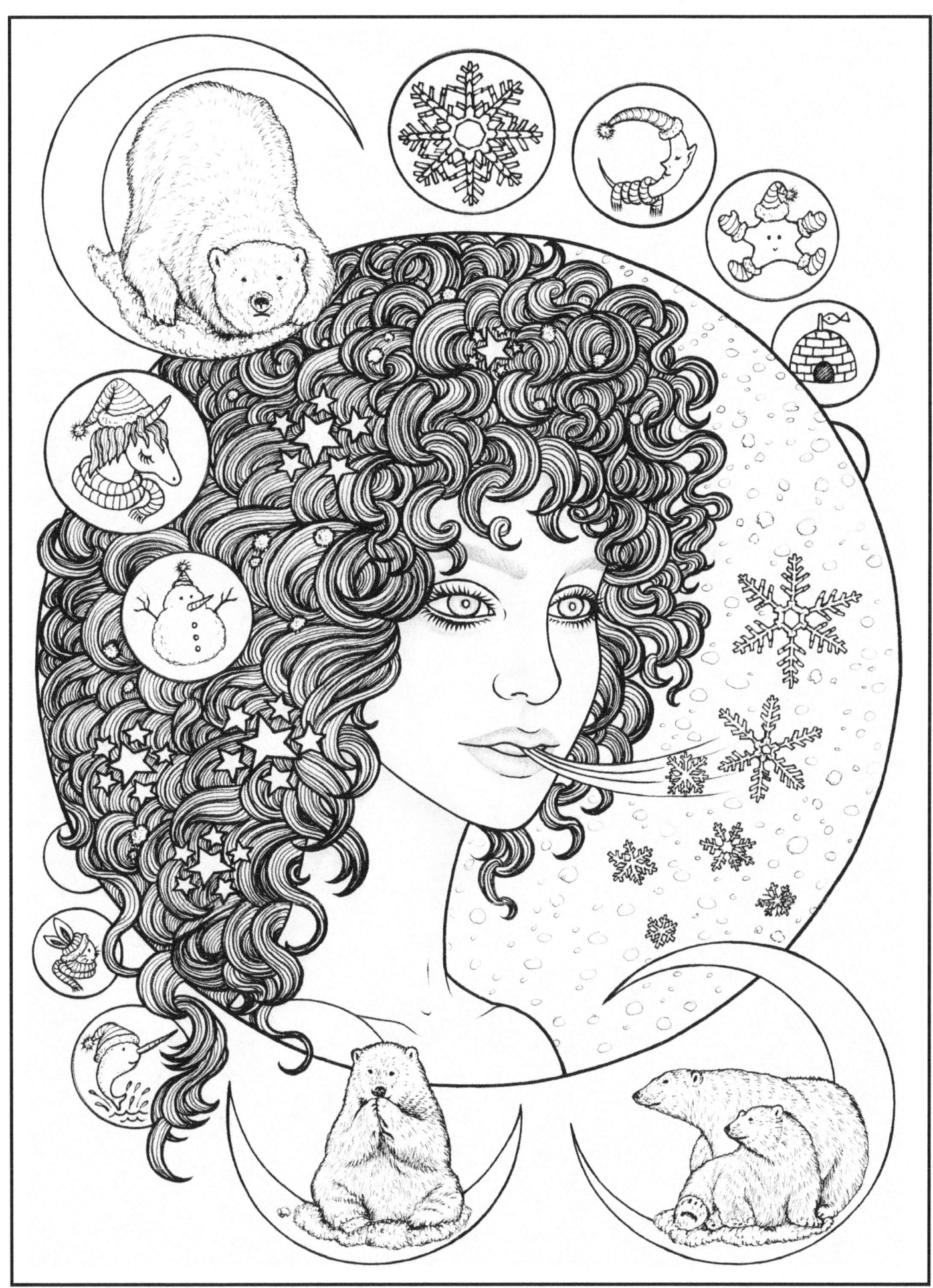

"Snow Queen" colored by:

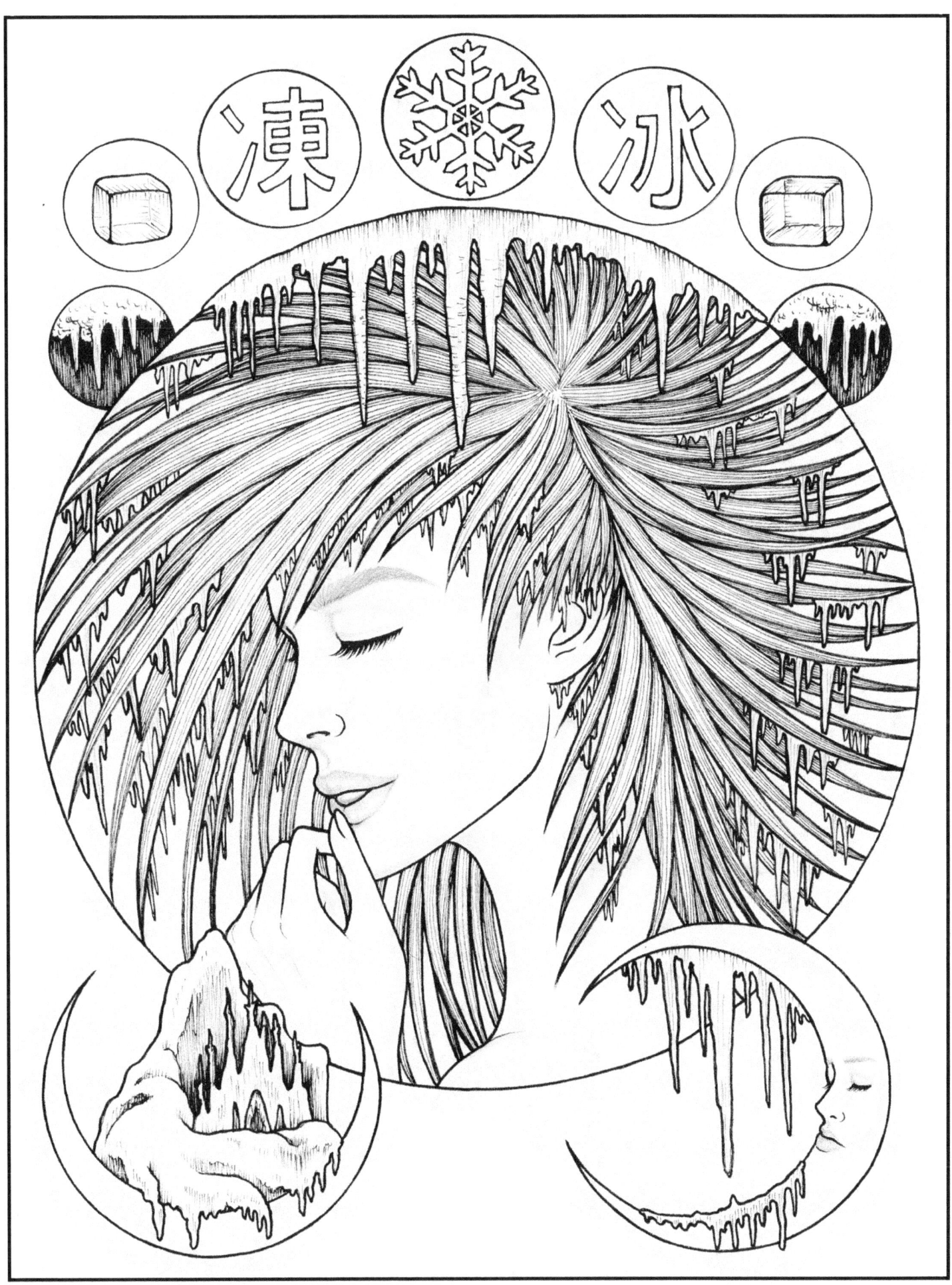

"Memory - A Place Frozen In Time" colored by:

© Wheeshan Ong

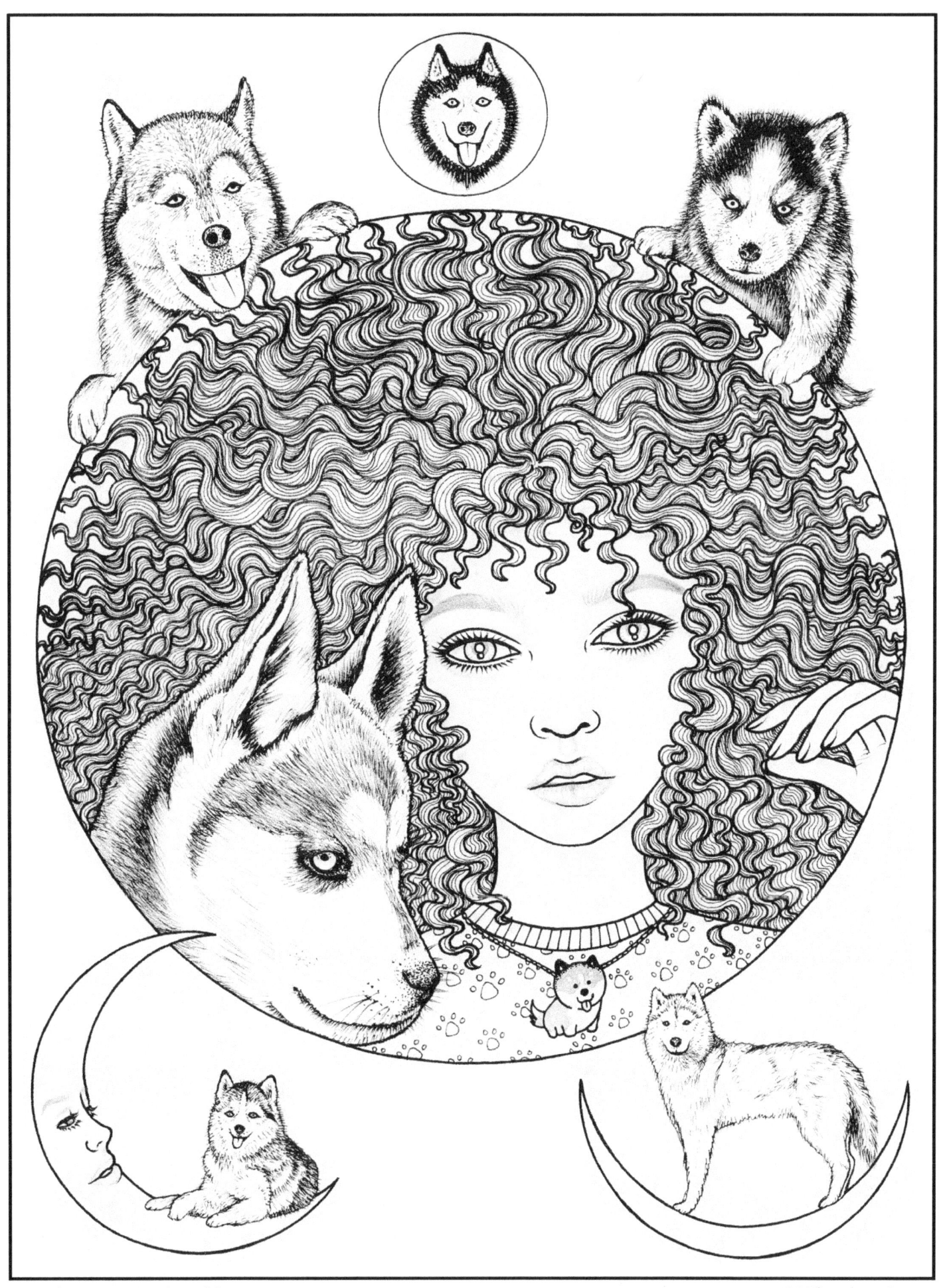

"Husky Moon" colored by:

© Wheeshan Ong

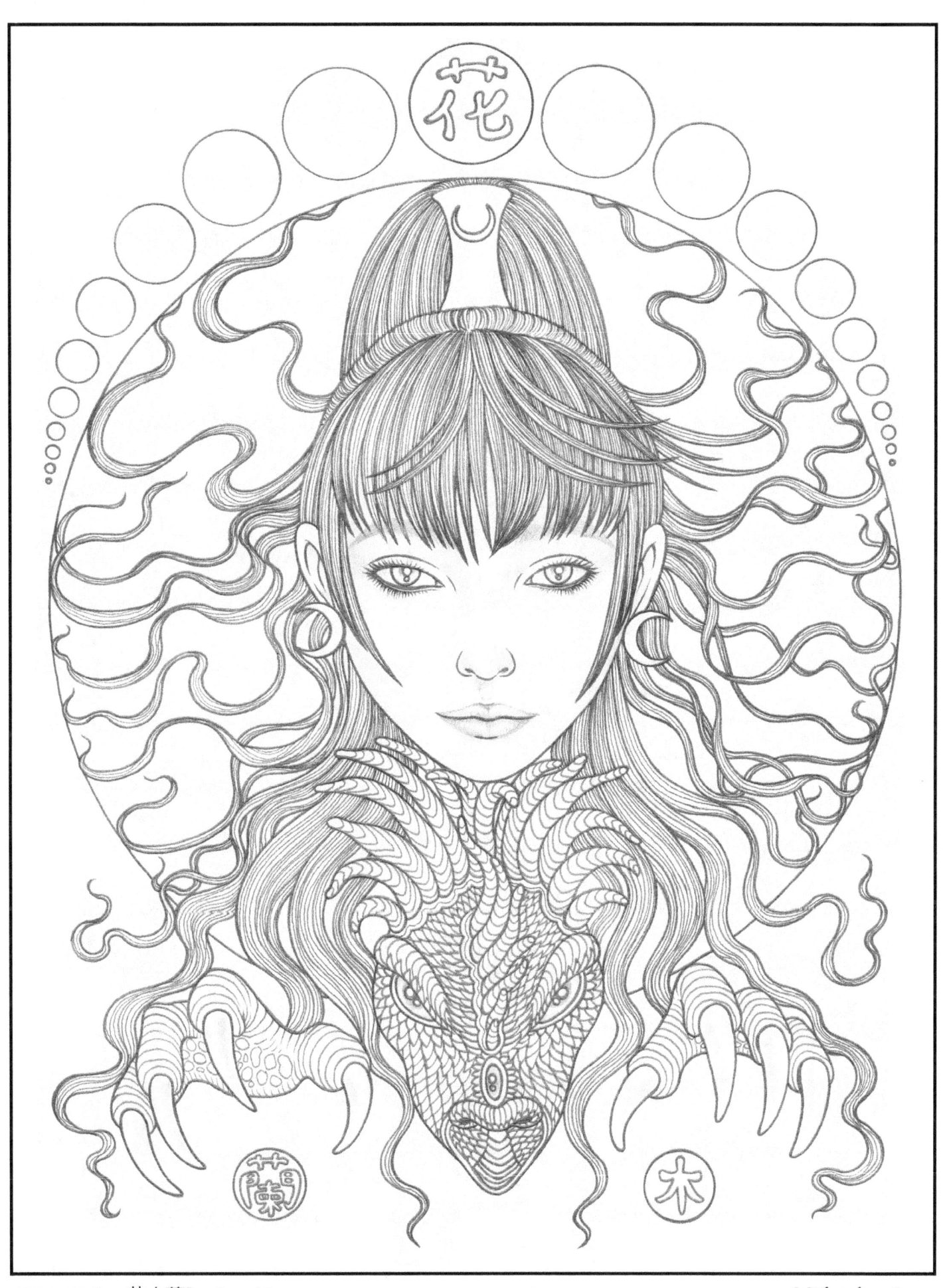

"Hua Mulan 花木蘭" colored by:

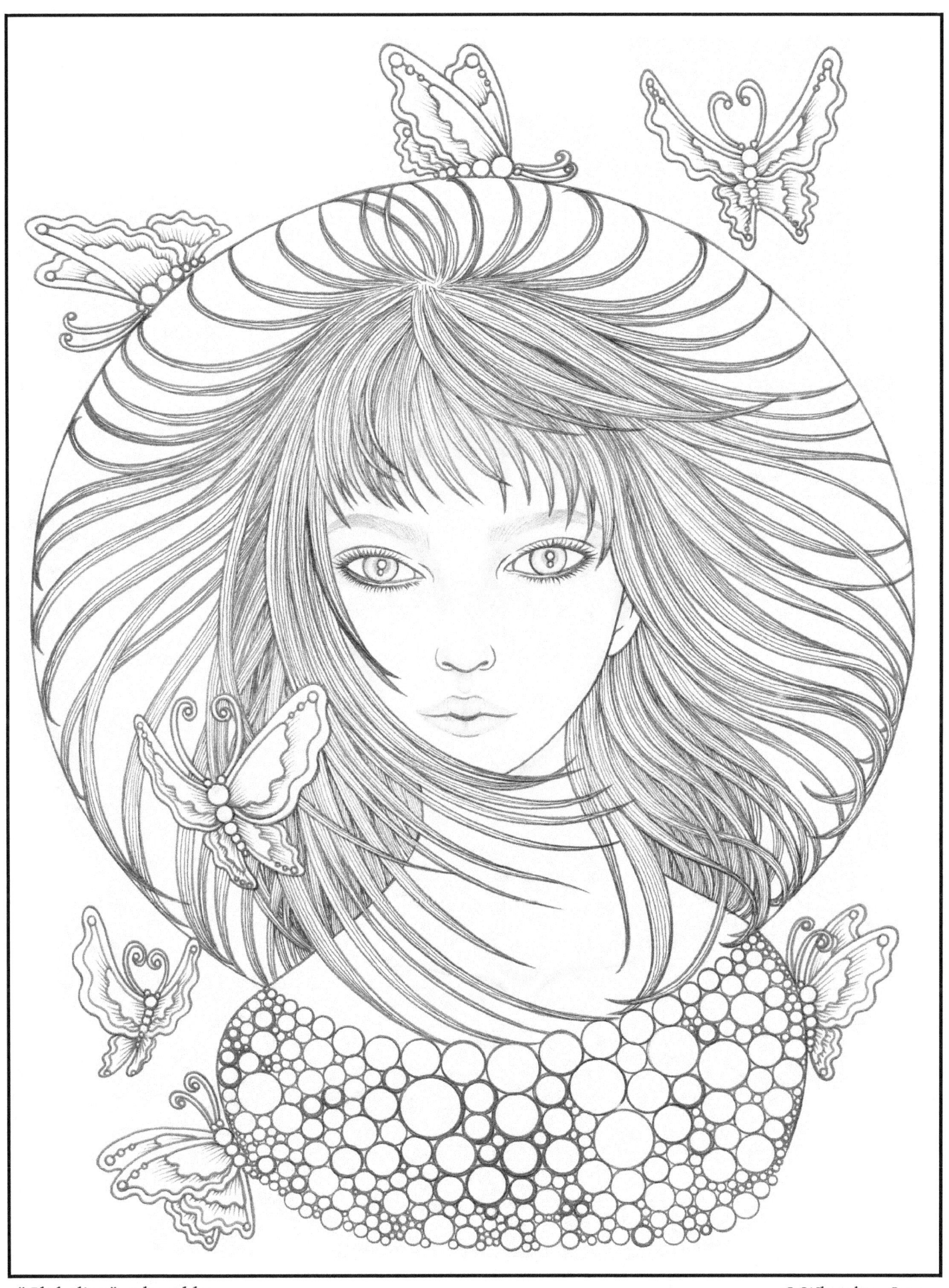

"Globelina" colored by:

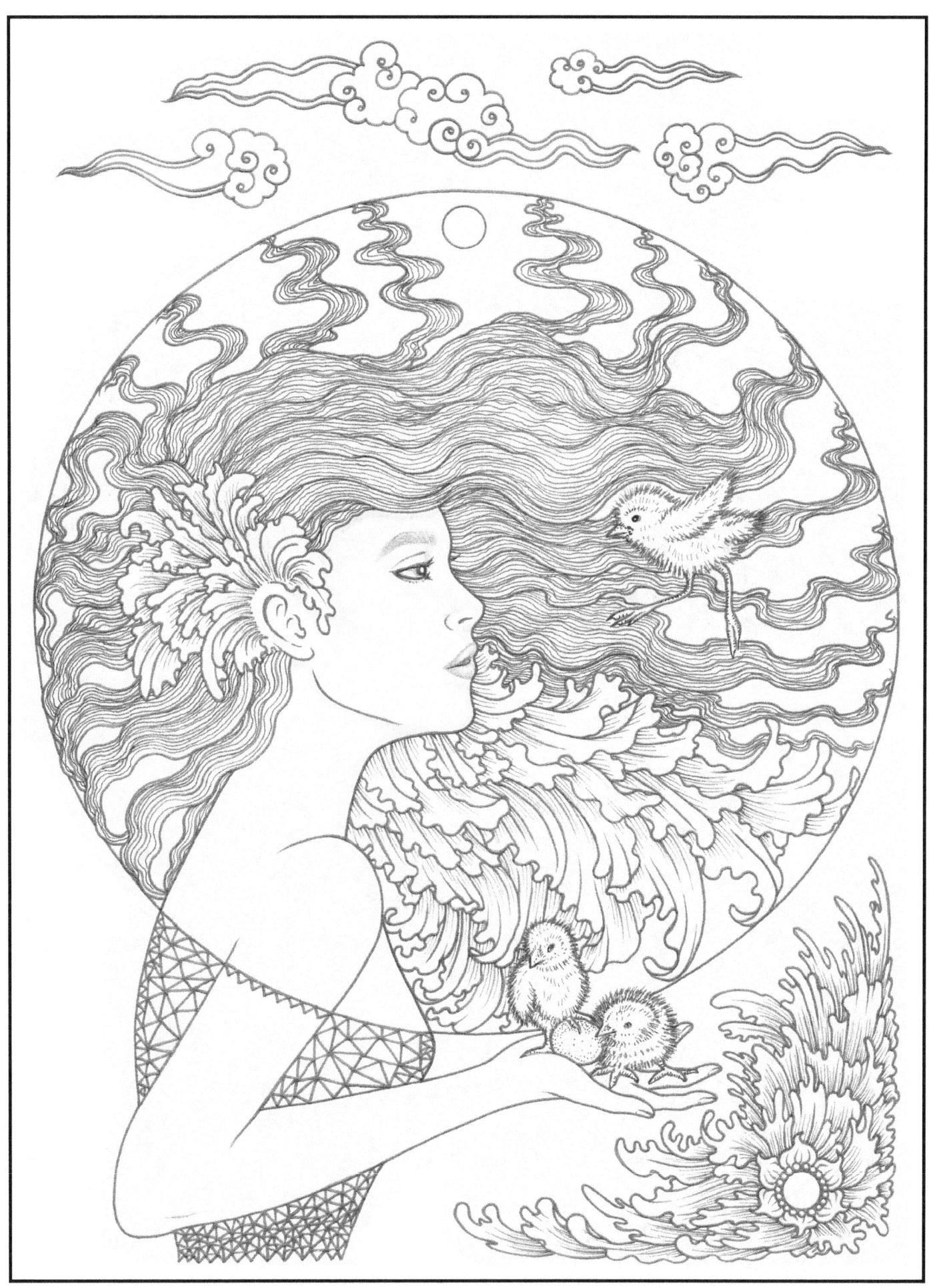

"Defy Gravity" colored by:

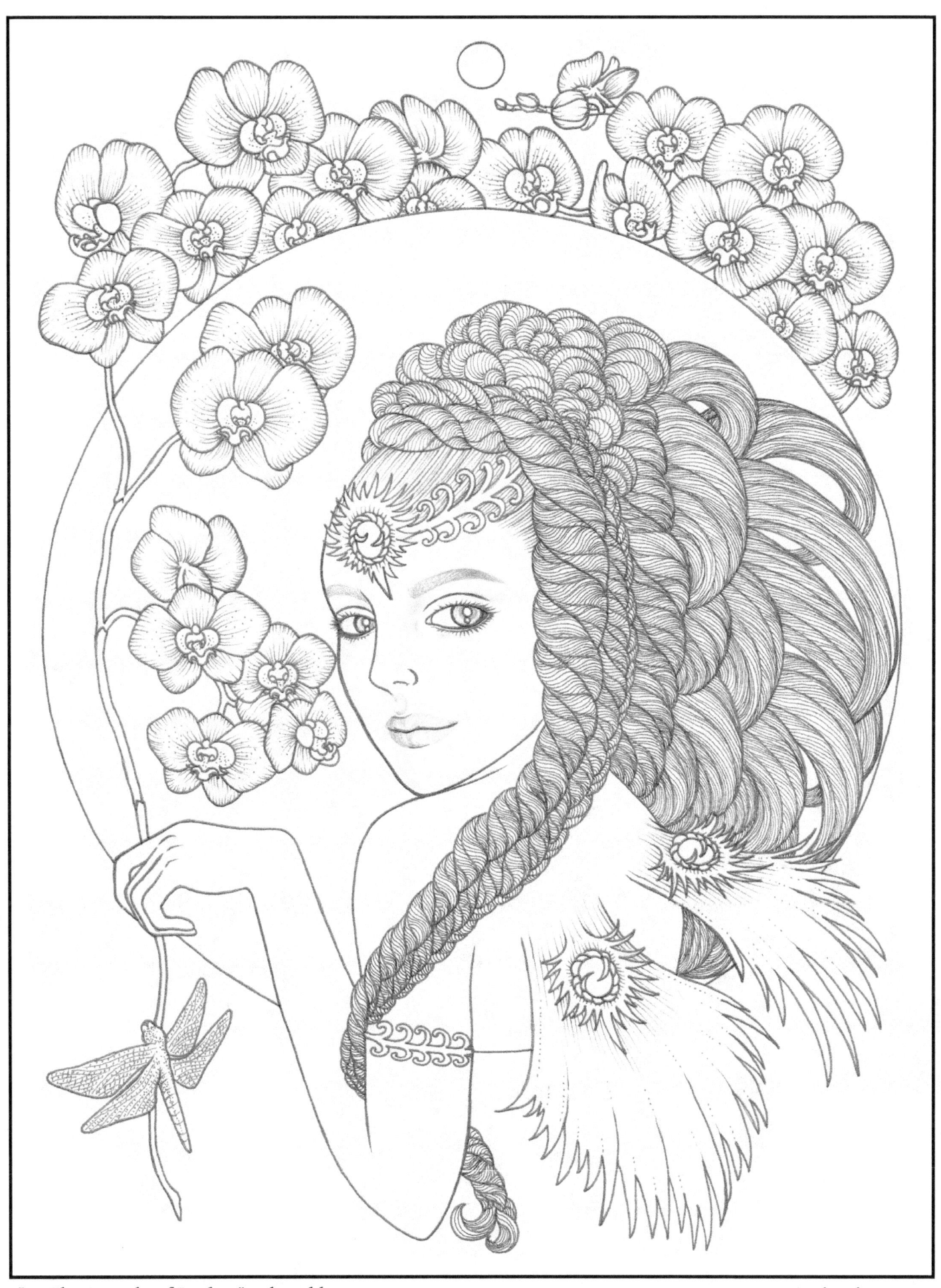

"In The Temple of Paphos" colored by:

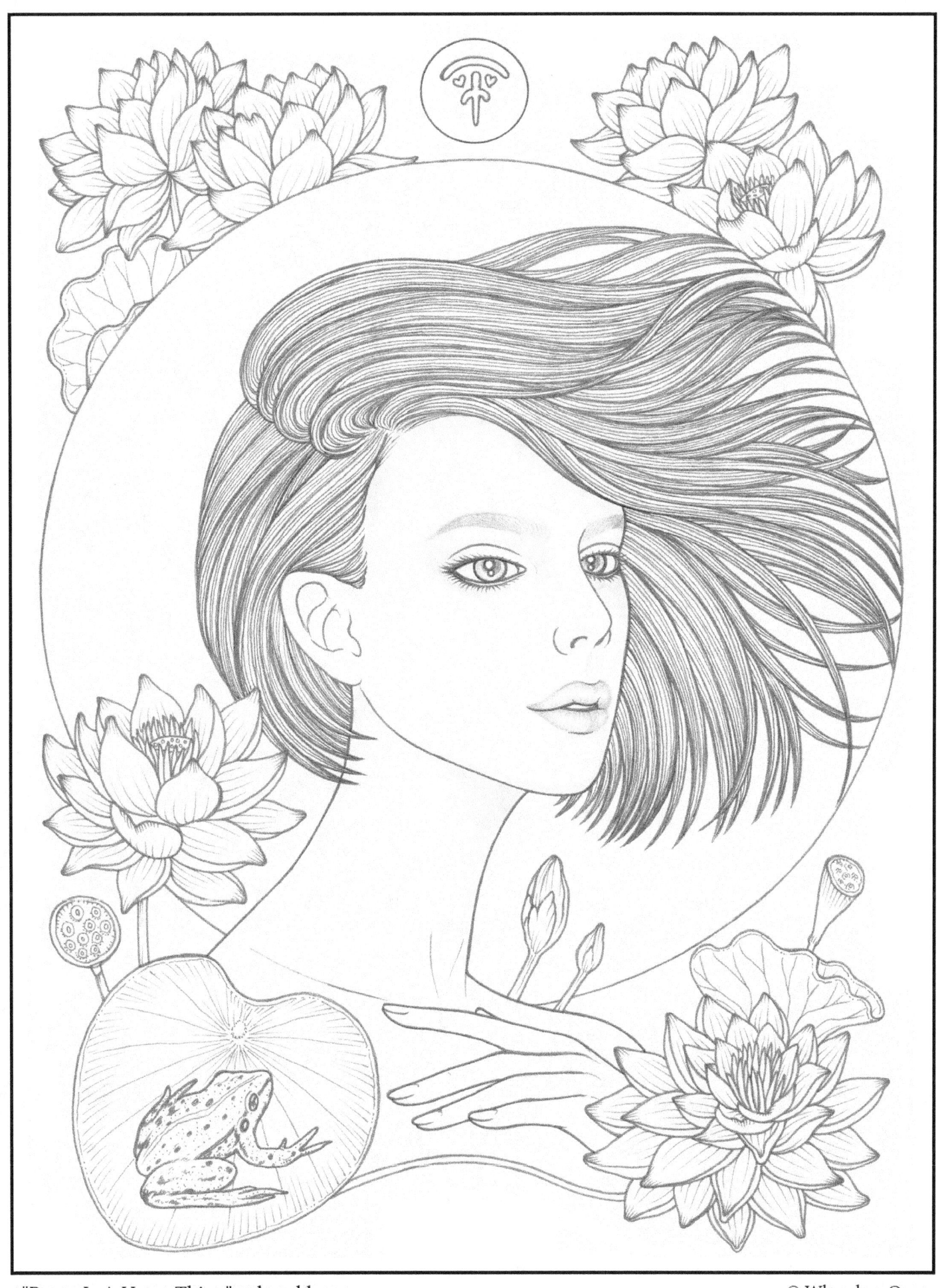

"Peace Is A Heart Thing" colored by:

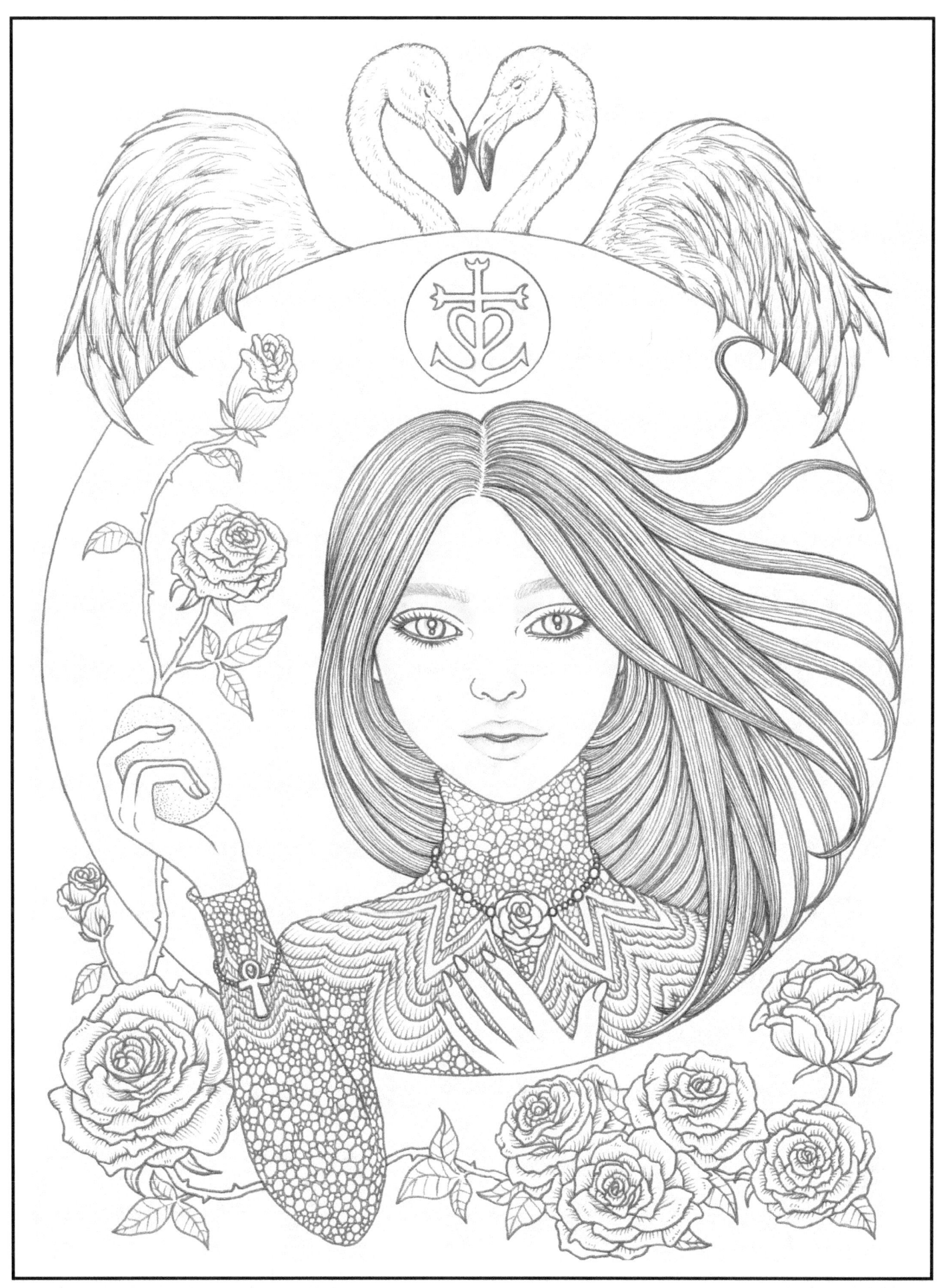

"In The Land of Camargue" colored by:

© Wheeshan Ong

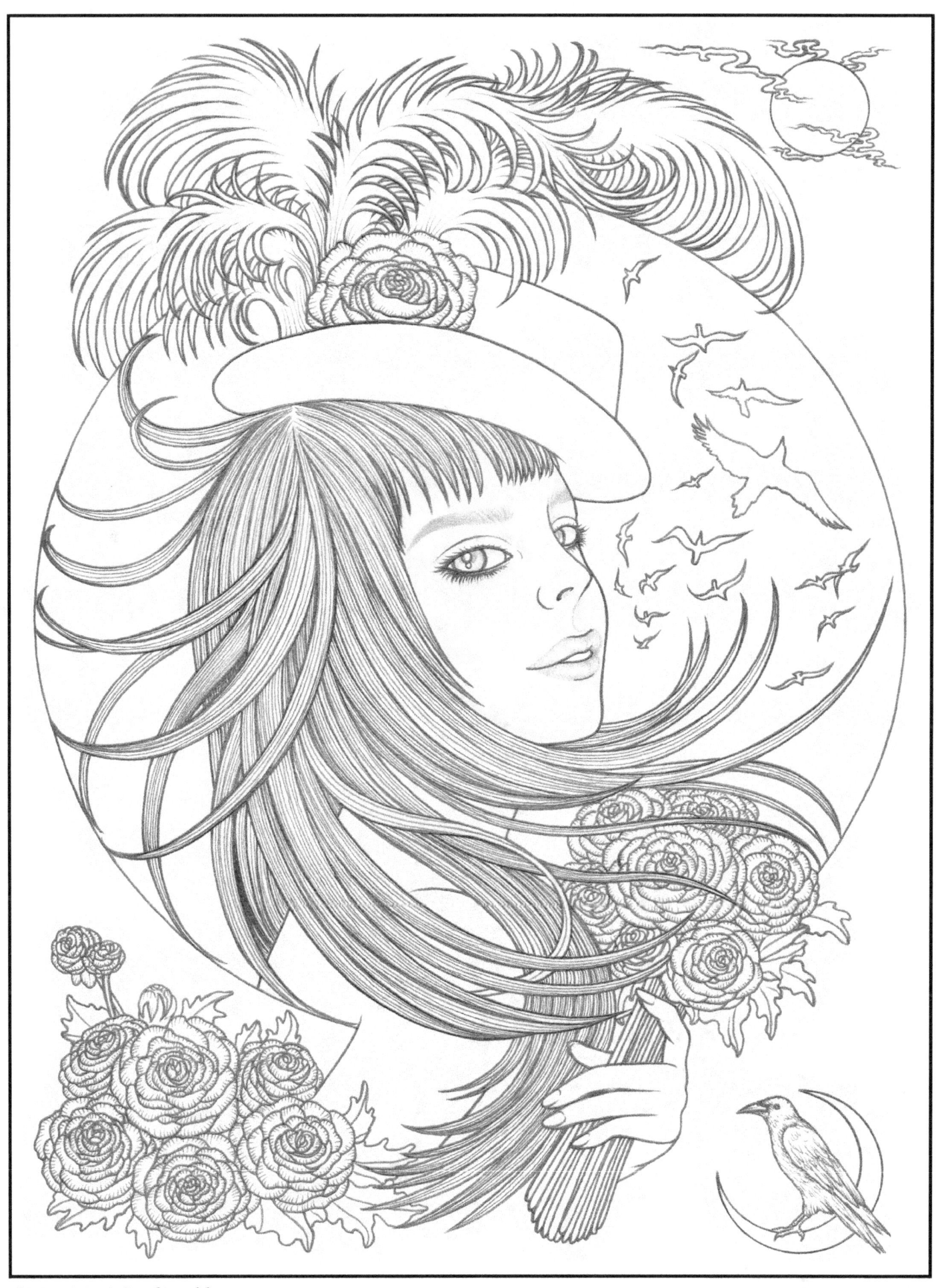

"I Am Magic" colored by:

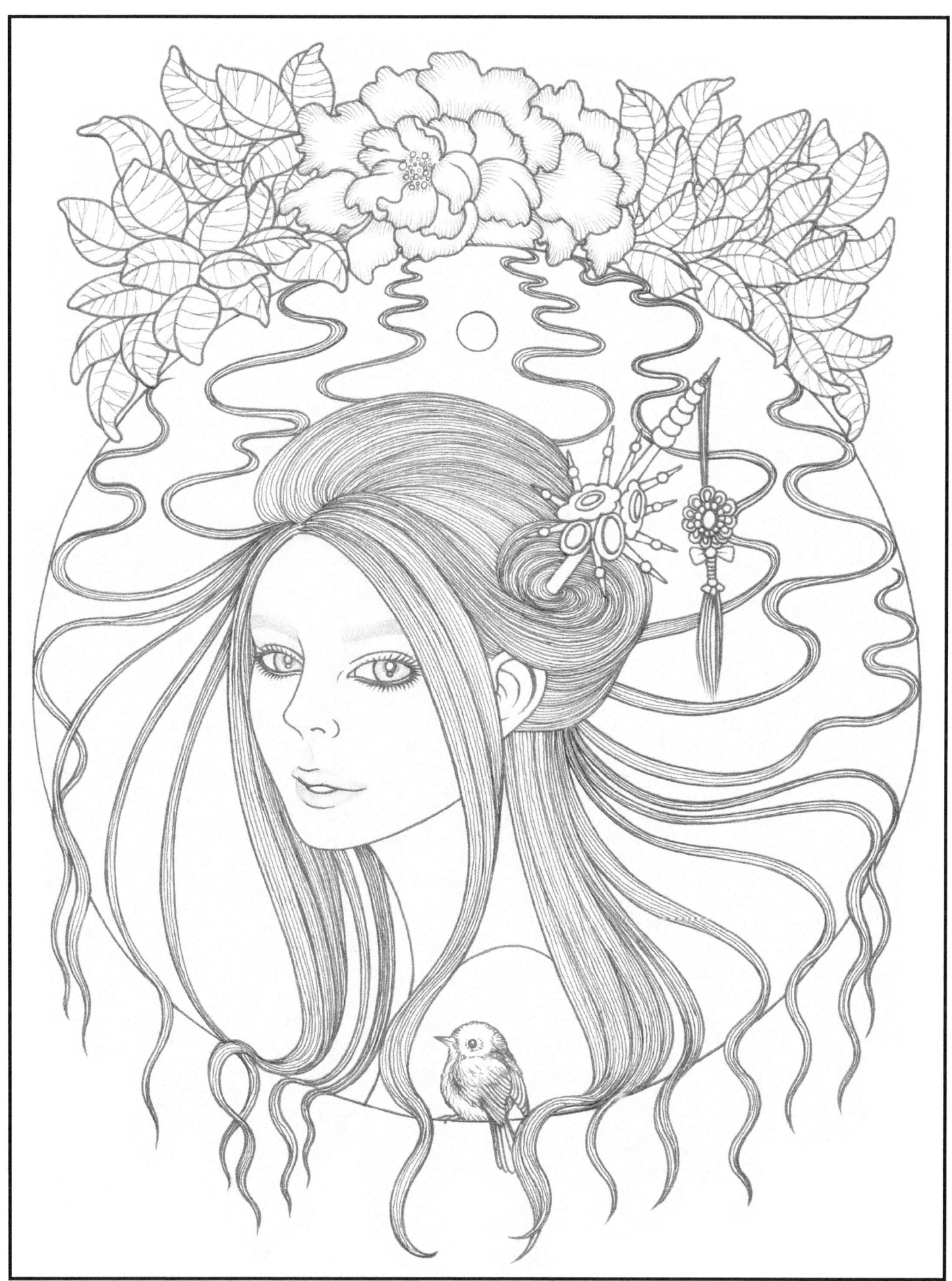

"Moon Is A Charmer" colored by:

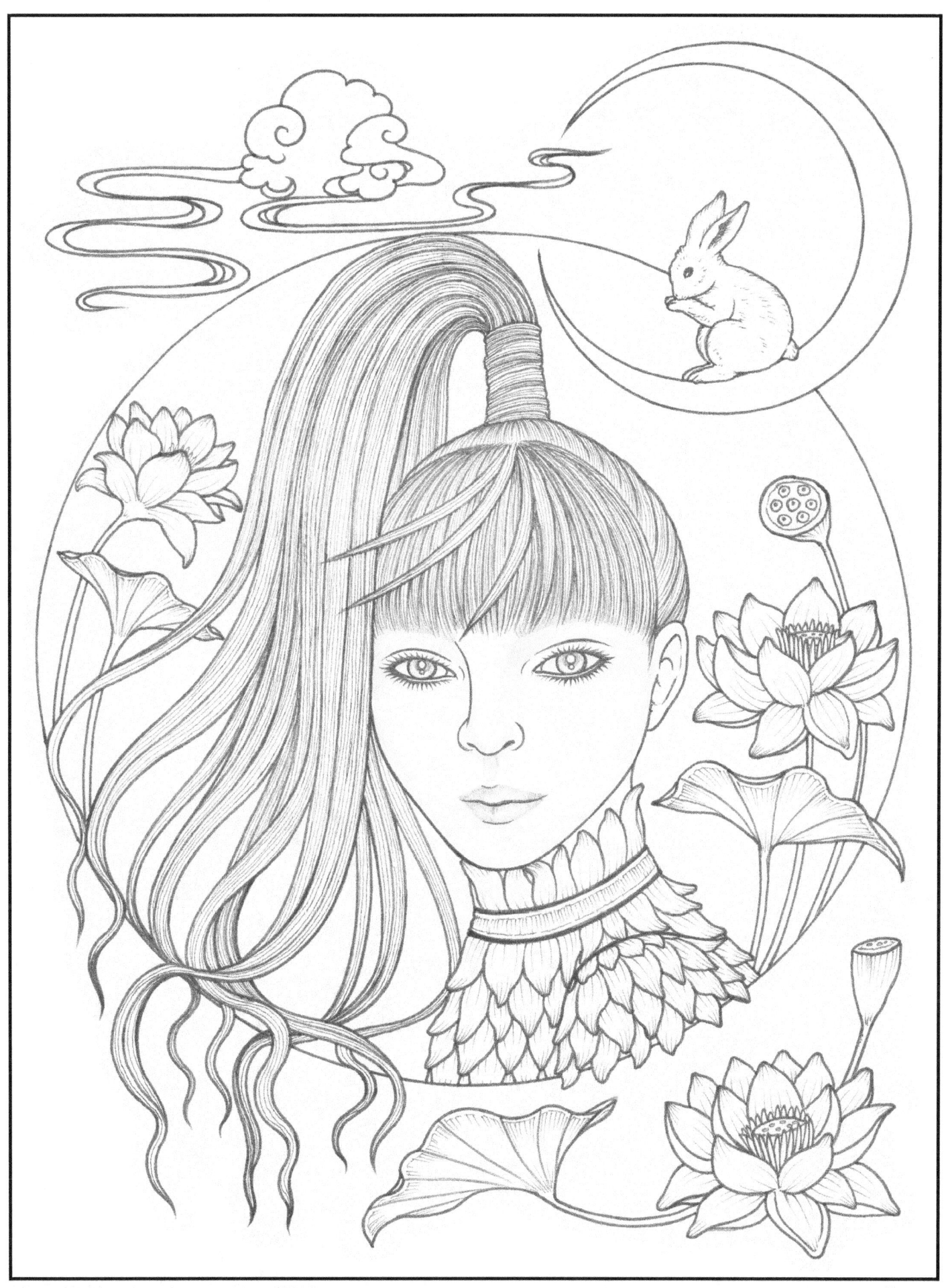

"Bunny On The Moon" colored by:

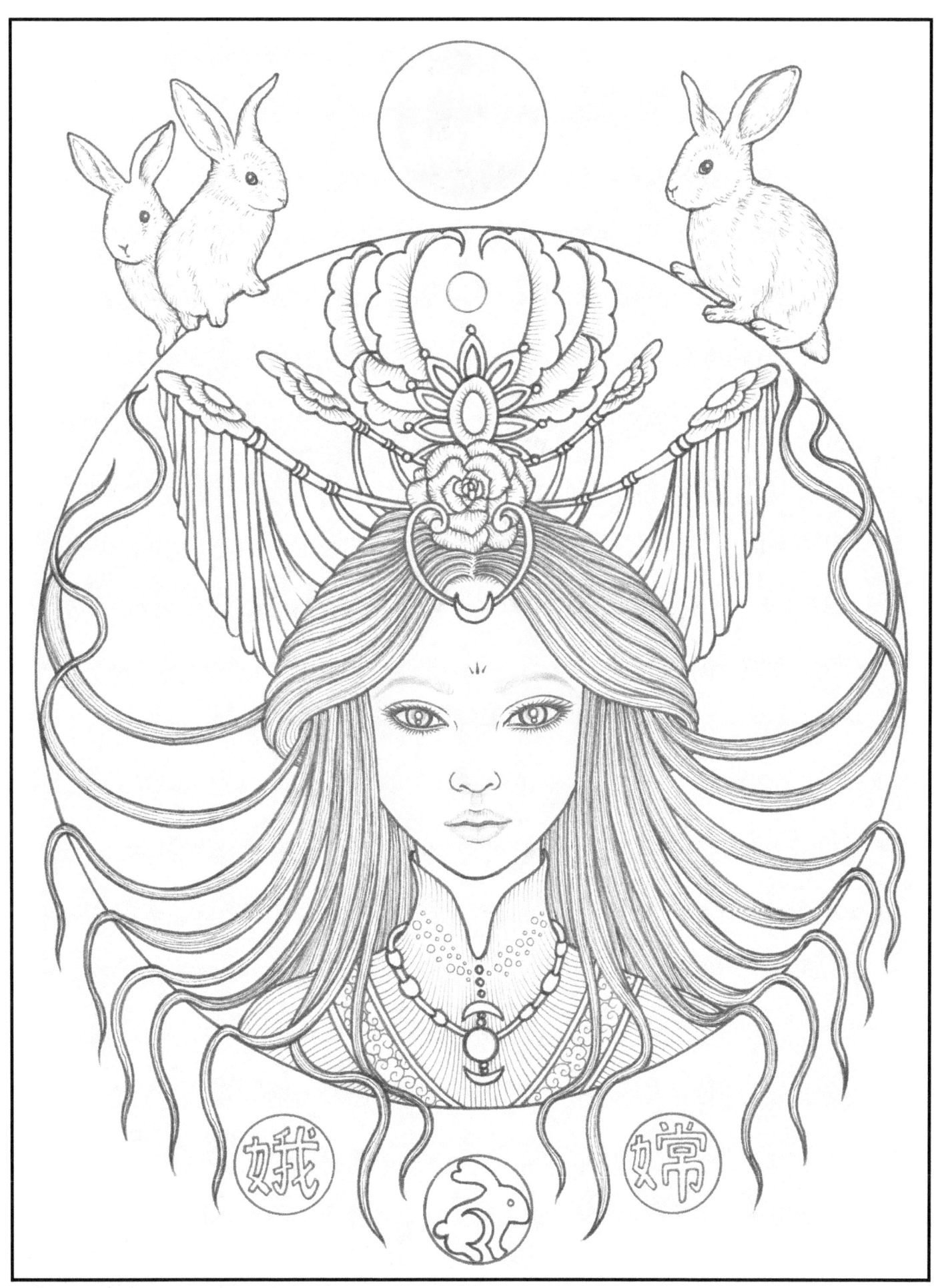

"Chang'e 嫦娥" colored by:

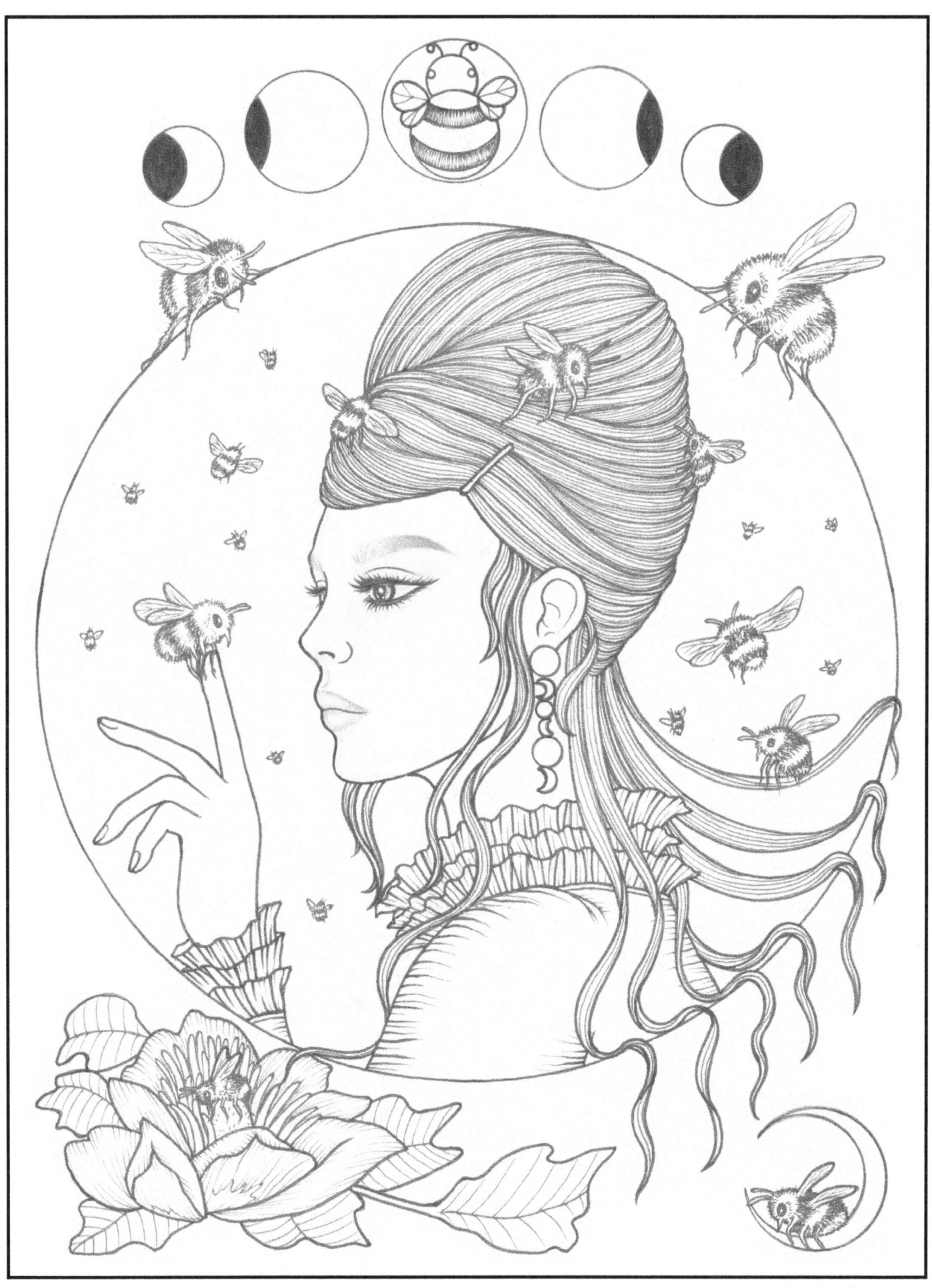

"Bumble Bella" colored by:

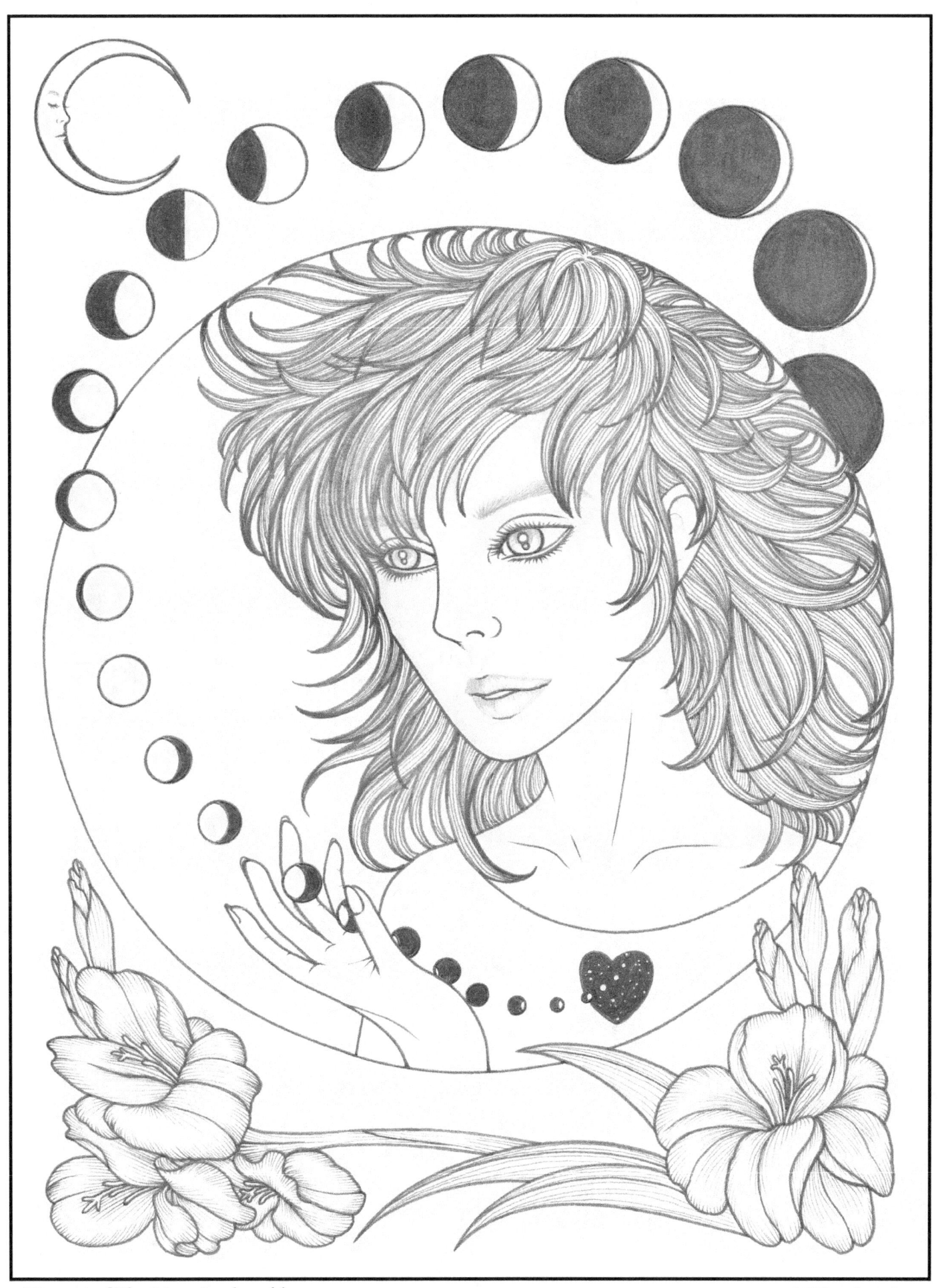

"Keeper of The Moon" colored by:

© Wheeshan Ong

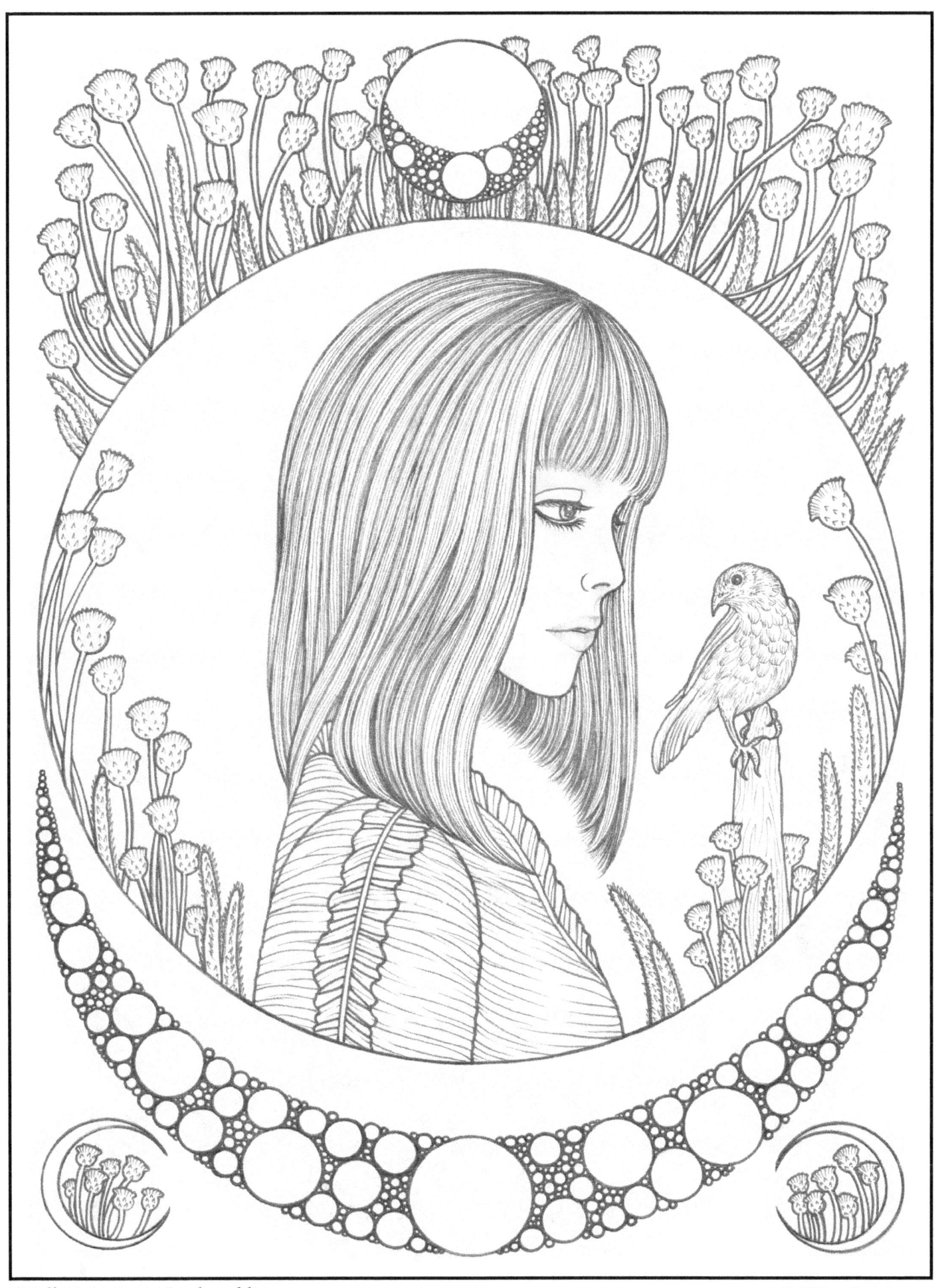

"Tell Me A Secret" colored by:

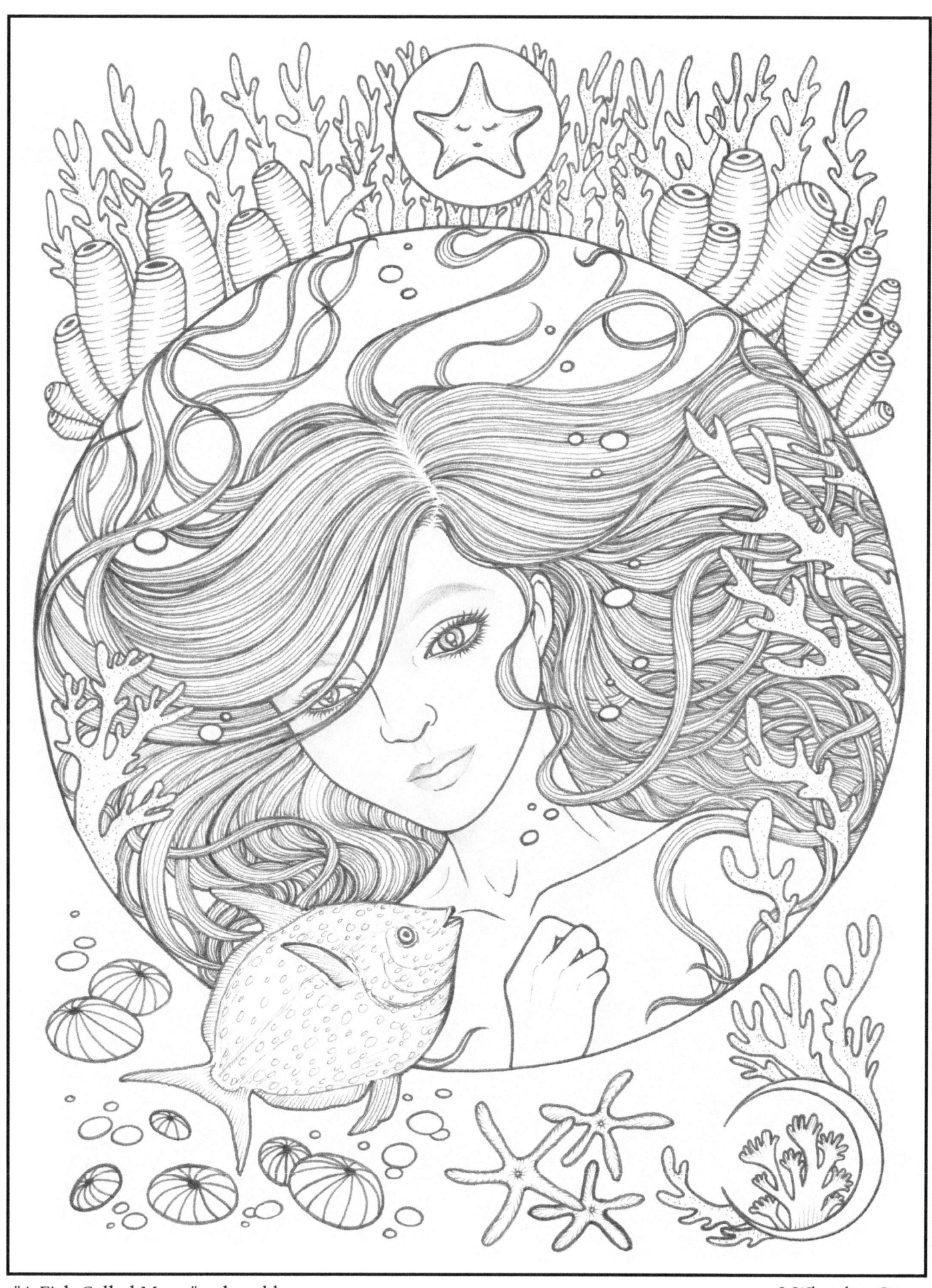

"A Fish Called Moon" colored by:

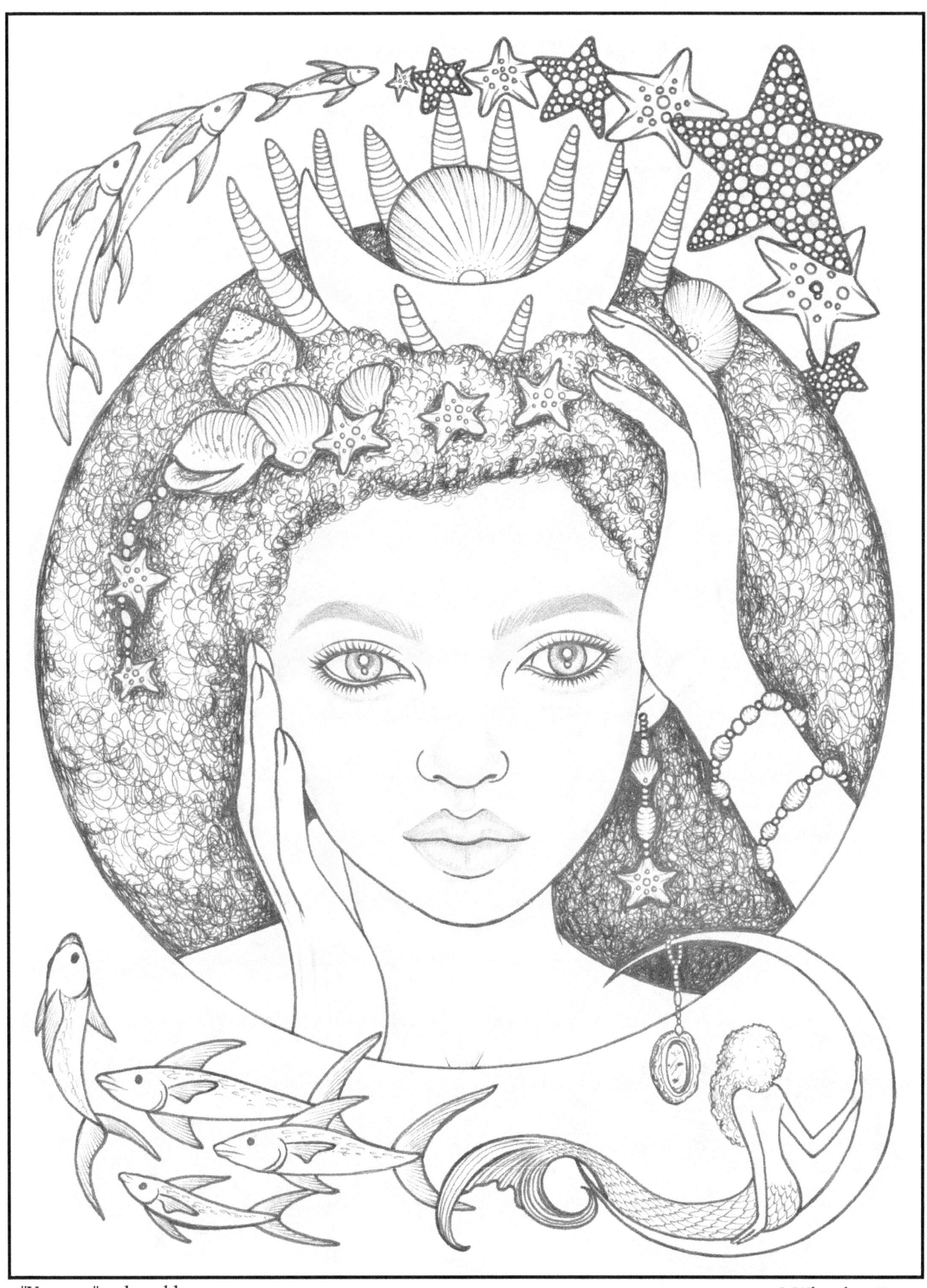

"Yemaya" colored by:

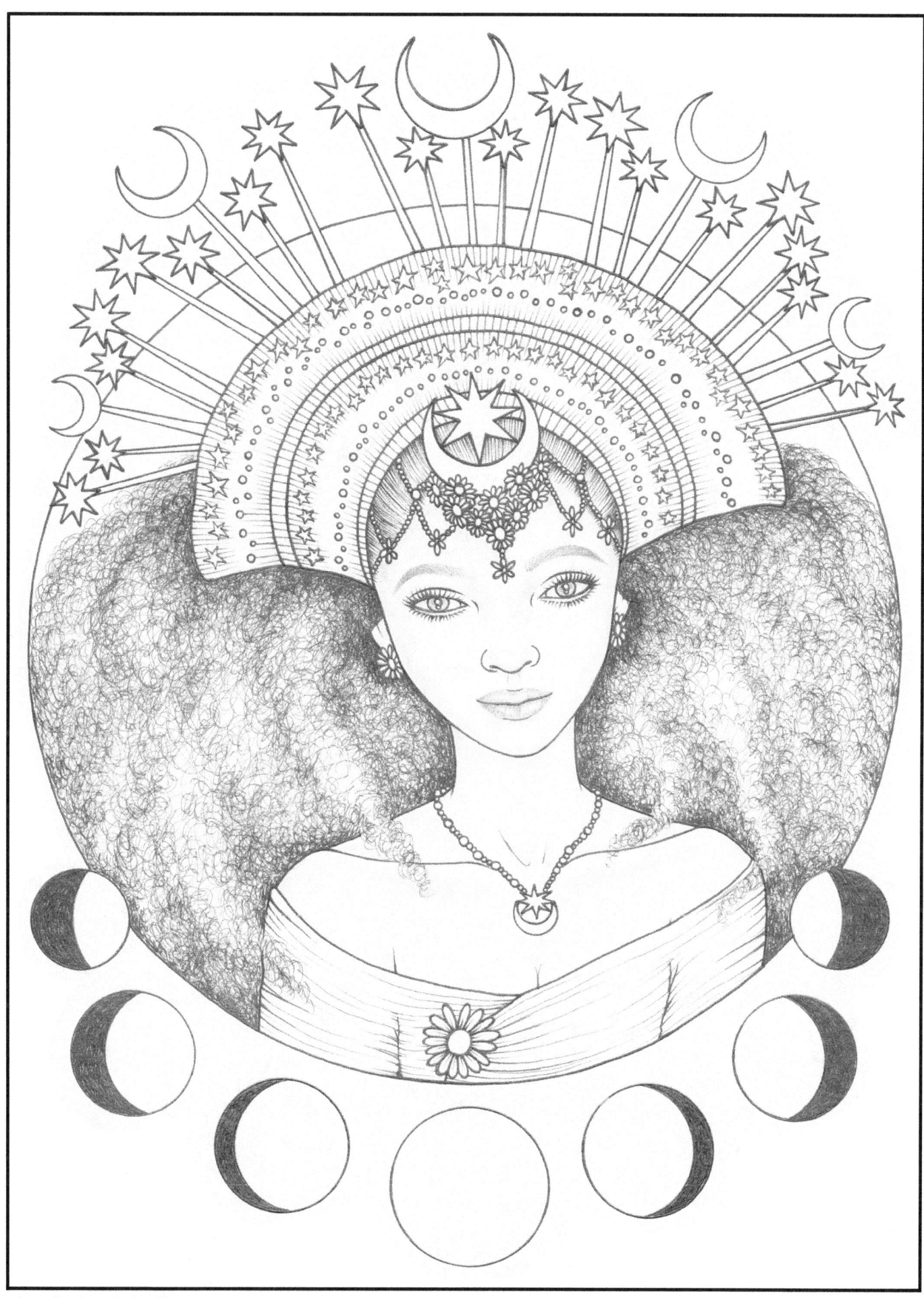

"Inanna" colored by:

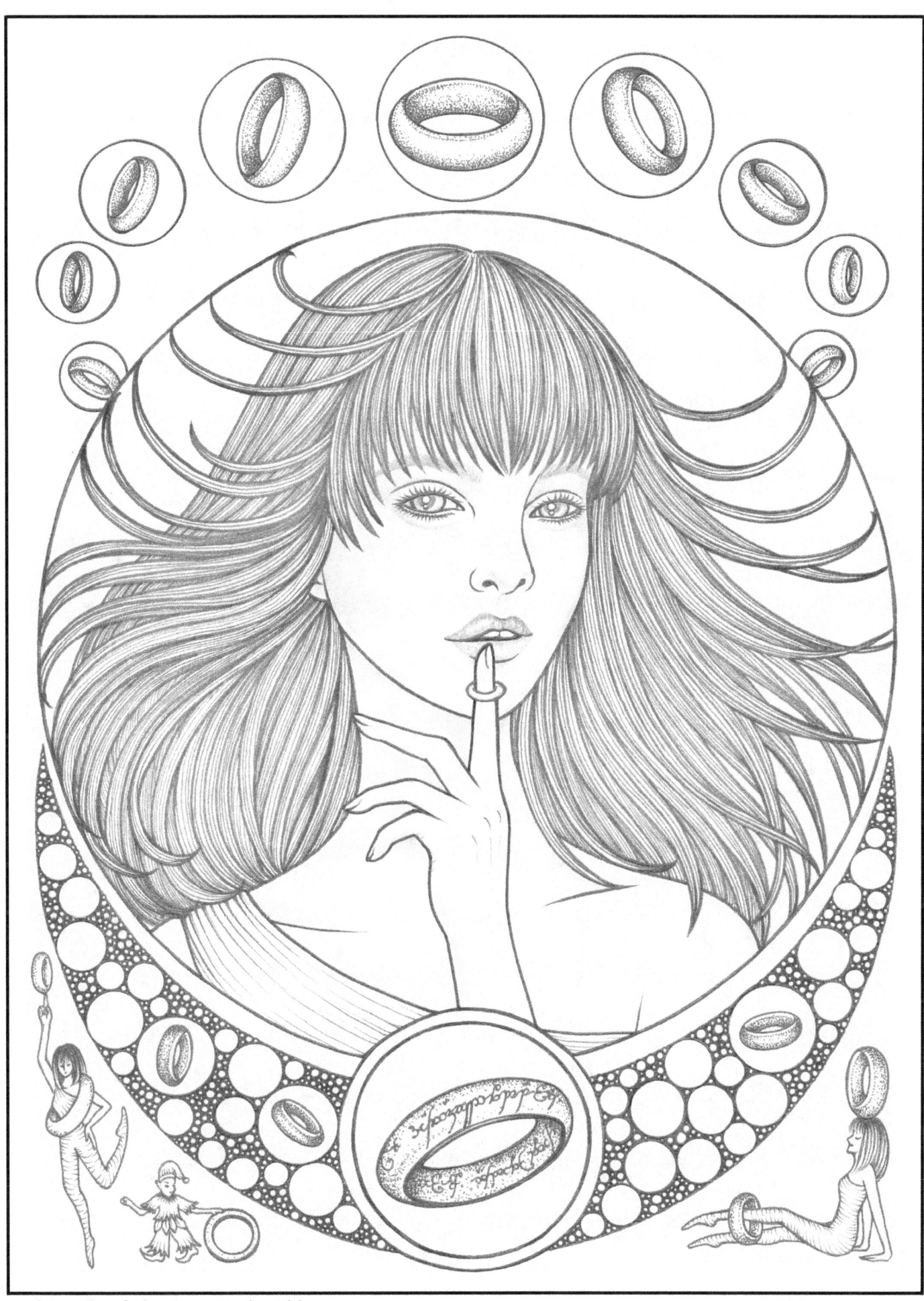

"The Lady of The Rings" colored by:

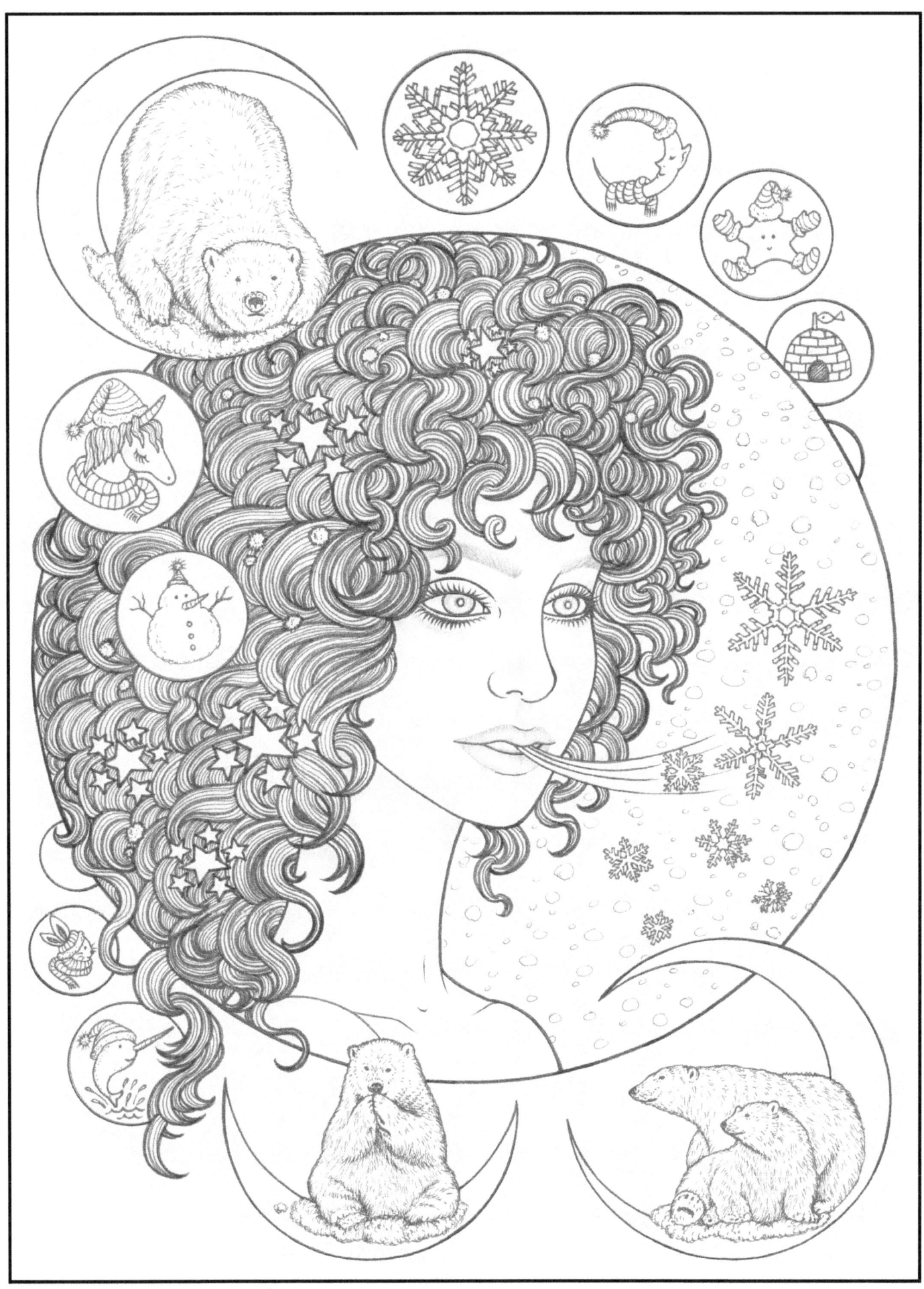

"Snow Queen" colored by:

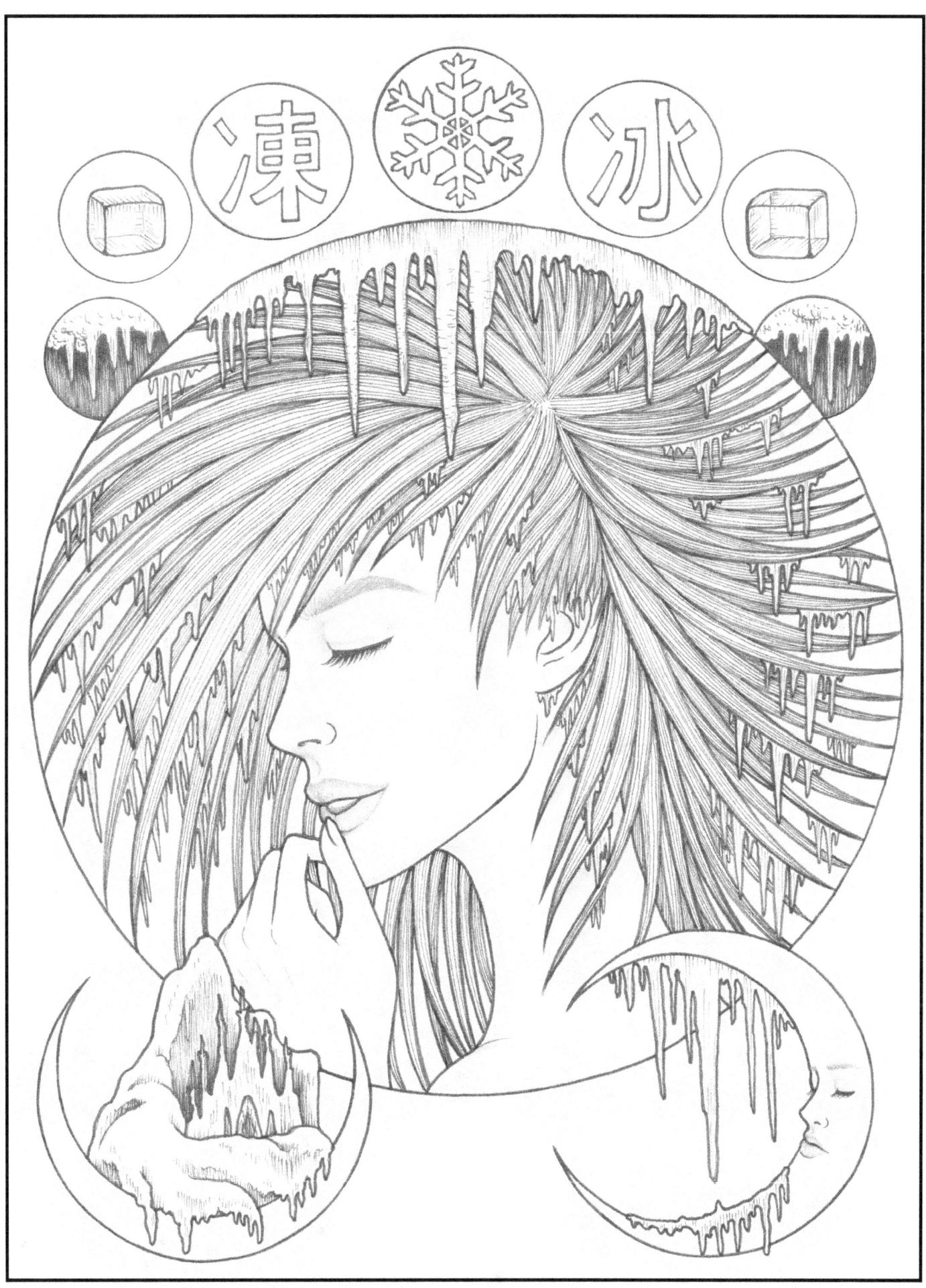

"Memory - A Place Frozen In Time" colored by:

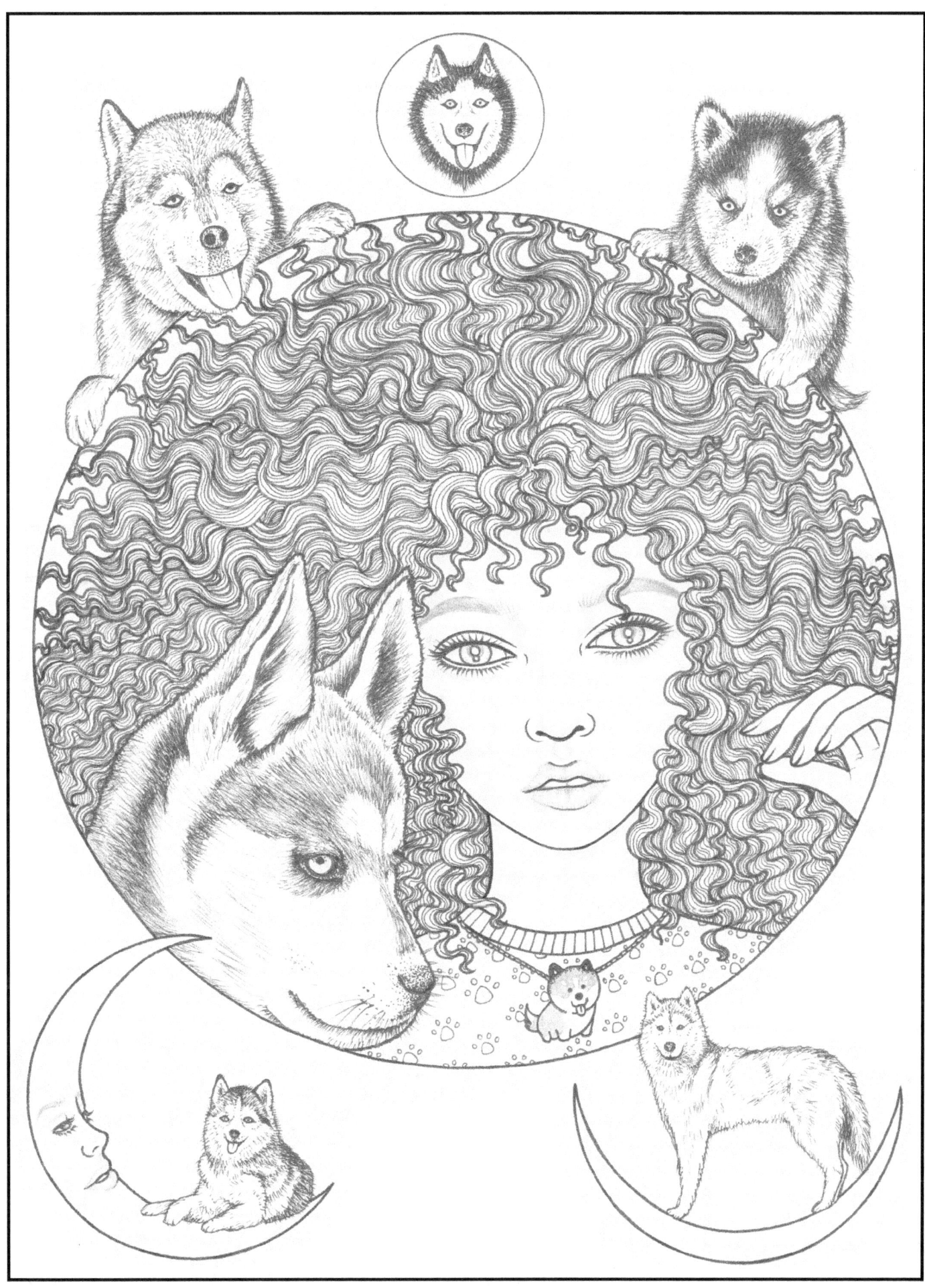

"Husky Moon" colored by:

www.ingramcontent.com/pod-product-compliance
Lightning Source LLC
Chambersburg PA
CBHW080850220526
45467CB00008B/2460